Praise for
To Protect and Maintain Individual Rights

The inspiring words of our Declaration of Rights, and sometimes less-inspiring court decisions which implement them, are the subject of this wonderful little book. To ensure our Declaration of Rights is not rendered, in the words of James Madison, a "mere demarcation on parchment," we must rely on an independent judiciary which, again in the words of Madison, "will be an impenetrable bulwark against every assumption of power in the legislature or executive." Since our constitution also provides we elect our judiciary, and ultimate sovereignty resides in our people, the wisdom of this book serves as a high standard against which we ought to judge our judges.

The Hon. Richard B. Sanders
Former Justice, Washington State Supreme Court

The seventy-five delegates who drafted and ratified Washington's Constitution on July 4, 1889, understood the need to carefully articulate the rights of our citizens—and just as importantly, to codify limits to the state government's authority to infringe on those rights. The Freedom Foundation should be commended for this clear guide to our constitution, providing a concise reference guide which will enable Washington's people, from whom the government derives its power, to guard their rights from future challenges.

Rob McKenna
Attorney General of Washington

To Protect and Maintain Individual Rights

To Protect and Maintain Individual Rights

A Citizen's Guide to the
Washington Constitution, Article I

Jonathan Bechtle and Michael Reitz

Foreword by
Associate Chief Justice Charles W. Johnson

Freedom Foundation
2011

Bechtle, Jonathan.

To protect and maintain individual rights : a citizen's guide to the Washington Constitution, Article I / Jonathan Bechtle and Michael Reitz ; foreword by Associate Chief Justice Charles W. Johnson. -- Rev. ed. -- Olympia, WA : Freedom Foundation, c2011.

p. ; cm.

ISBN: 978-0-9835440-0-5

Revision of the 2008 ed. published by EFF Productions.

Includes bibliographical references.

1. Constitutions--Washington (State) 2. Constitutional law--Washington (State) 3. Civil rights--Washington (State) 4. Civil rights--United States. I. Reitz, Michael. II. Title.

KFW401 1889 .A6 2011

342.79702--dc22   1109

Published in the United States by:
Freedom Foundation
P.O. Box 552
Olympia, WA 98507
wwww.myfreedomfoundation.com

Manufactured in the United States of America

Cover photo: the Legislative Building at the Washington State Capitol, Olympia, Washington

Contents

Foreword

History is often a great teacher. However, unless one is exposed to historical sources, learning about and appreciating fundamental principles rooted in our history proves difficult. Such is the case with our state constitution; the rights, privileges and duties established under the provisions crafted more than a century ago. The more we know about these constitutional principles, the better we understand and appreciate our constitutionally based form of government.

Jonathan Bechtle and Michael Reitz, the authors of this *Citizen's Guide to the Washington Constitution, Article I,* asked me to review this work and offer an opening comment to this book. I am happy to do so. As a justice on the Washington State Supreme Court for, as of this writing, almost eighteen years, I often enjoy the opportunity to conduct historical research on constitutional issues, attempting to decipher the words chosen by the drafters and interpret the meaning of those words in the context of the legal issue the court is faced with resolving. That is part of my responsibilities as a justice on the court. But I have the benefit of the arguments of the attorneys in the case, the decision and record from the court ruling under review, and a wealth of resource materials regularly available to me. Citizens often lack ready access to such materials. This citizen's guide provides another readily available resource summarizing and discussing individual constitutional provisions, their meaning and relevance to our lives.

For almost fourteen years, I have taught a survey course on the Washington State Constitution at Seattle University Law School. I know and appreciate the incredible amount of thought, research and work necessary to produce this citizen's guide. The authors are to be commended for their efforts in putting this work together. Those who read and use this guide can be thankful for the time and energy spent on organizing and publishing it.

Reading about and understanding our constitutional foundations is somewhat akin to political speech and debate. The more one can learn and understand the principles involved, the better informed and educated one becomes. And, hopefully, results in a higher degree of appreciation toward our constitutionally based form of government.

This guide concerns those provisions articulated under Article I, our declaration of rights. Our state constitution contains more articles dealing with subjects such as our legislative authority and initiatives and referenda, the executive authority, limitations on taxation and debt, education, and others. More research and reading is necessary to fully appreciate the constitutional foundations of our state government. This guide provides an excellent exposure to those rights we all enjoy as citizens.

Charles W. Johnson
Associate Chief Justice
Washington State Supreme Court

Introduction

On July 4, 1889, a convention of seventy-five delegates gathered in Olympia, Washington, to compose a state constitution. These lawyers, judges, doctors, teachers, politicians, and businessmen had the benefit of observing the constitutions of numerous other states when drafting Washington's governing document. After forty days of deliberation—sometimes fierce, sometimes collegial—the delegates formally adopted the constitution. Understanding these debates, and their context, is critical for citizens to properly exercise and safeguard their rights.

The first principle articulated in Washington's constitution is its source of authority. Individual citizens are endowed with inherent freedoms that can neither be conferred nor exterminated by the state. The constitution, then, is a delegation of authority from the state's sovereigns—the citizens—to the separate branches of government.

Indeed, the opening section of the Washington Constitution declares: "All political power is inherent in the people, and governments derive their just powers from the consent of the governed, and are established to protect and maintain individual rights" (Art. I § 1). Theodore L. Stiles, a convention delegate and original justice of the Supreme Court of Washington, once wrote that the constitution is an "instrument of limitation." That is, the constitution serves to limit the branches of government, rather than conferring unlimited power.

The first article in the constitution is the Declaration of Rights, which catalogs the fundamental liberties granted by the "Supreme Ruler of the Universe." The constitution does not grant these rights to citizens, but recognizes the rights with the goal of protecting them from government encroachment. These fundamental rights, however, cannot be exercised or preserved if the sovereigns lose sight of them. A recent study showed that Americans were more familiar with the characters of a popular television cartoon than with the freedoms identified in the First Amendment. If familiarity with the U.S. Constitution is lacking, awareness of the provisions of the state constitution is deplorable. This is unfortunate.

As Justice Robert F. Utter wrote in 1991, state constitutions were originally intended to be the first line of defense for the protection of individual liberty, with the federal Constitution acting as a secondary protection. As a result, state constitutions were intended to extend broader protections to citizens. In the seminal case *State v. Gunwall* (1986), the Supreme Court of Washington recognized that the Washington Constitution may often extend broader rights to its citizens than the U.S. Constitution, and the court provided criteria for analyzing specific situations. This evaluation necessitates a careful comparison of the constitutional texts and the history behind specific provisions.

Sadly, while minutes of motions and votes were recorded during the Washington convention, a complete record of the proceedings does not exist. The delegates had secured the services of court reporters who kept a verbatim record of convention debates and speeches. When the legislature failed to appropriate payment for their services, the stenographers destroyed their records. Legal practitioners and researchers are left with the delegates' subsequent writings, contemporary newspaper accounts of the convention, and the minutes of the proceedings, which are published in the *Journal of the Washington State Convention, 1889.*

Because of the lack of historical documents, we compiled this guide as a reference tool for citizens—particularly those who wish to hold their elected representatives accountable. When citizens are educated in the sources of their freedoms, and familiar with attempts in history to limit these freedoms, they are better equipped to recognize new encroachments. We hope this guide will help illuminate the constitutional provisions that recognize and guarantee our inherent rights.

The Washington Constitution counsels us that a "frequent recurrence to fundamental principles is essential to the security of individual right and the perpetuity of free government" (Art. I § 32). This admonishment is appropriate not only for lawmakers and judges, but for all those who love liberty and seek to preserve it. Our system of free government is founded by the consent of the governed, and it requires frequent, vigilant review to secure our continued prosperity.

As Ronald Reagan warned, "Freedom is never more than one generation away from extinction. We didn't pass it to our children in the bloodstream. It must be fought for, protected, and handed on to them to do the same, or one day we will spend our sunset years telling our children and our children's children what it was once like in the United States where men were free."

Preamble to the Washington Constitution

We, the people of the state of Washington, grateful to the Supreme Ruler of the Universe for our liberties, do ordain this constitution.

Flowery hyperbole, dire warnings of communism, "buffoonish" comments, and delegates pale-faced with anger stalking out of the hall: such was the scene at Washington's constitutional convention on July 30, 1889, the day the delegates discussed the preamble. The conflict didn't arise because anyone opposed having a preamble or because of any difference of opinion over its purpose. The argument centered on an amendment offered by Seattle delegate Trusten Dyer to insert a mention of "Almighty God" in the middle of the first draft of the preamble, which had not mentioned the Deity.

That motion brought a storm of rhetoric, from both those who supported the idea as reflective of Washingtonians' values and those who opposed it as mere sentimentality that had no place in a business document.

Lawyer George Comegys opposed Dyer's amendment, because "the preamble should briefly state the facts," to which Judge Turner from Spokane Falls replied that, while he admitted the mention of God was purely a matter of sentiment, "[I]t accords with the sentiments of ninety-nine out of every hundred citizens of Washington." Democratic Delegate Godman retorted, "if 999 people asked to have anything done for sentiment and one opposed it on principle, he would stand by the man of principle" (*Globe,* July 30). And so went the morning. Even the reporters in attendance grew tired of the lengthy speeches on what seemed a minor issue, making a call for the "orators to be muzzled" (*Globe*, Aug. 1).

Despite the many speeches and frayed tempers, the delegates did not deadlock on this issue. Instead, they sent the preamble back to a committee to be reworked. The committee returned it on August 1 in the form of a majority report with no mention of God and a minority report including Him. The delegates were careful this time to curtail debate and quickly accepted the minority report as the final language.

No matter which side of this debate a delegate was on, there was unanimous concern for how every word of the constitution would affect future generations. Delegates wanted a workable document that reflected the views of their constituents, even for seemingly unimportant clauses, such as the preamble. When Delegate Sullivan called the addition of God "all for show" and "stuff and nonsense," he recognized the same truth as the delegates who argued that not including God would seem "indirect pandering to infidelity" to the people and would set "a bad example for the youth of the new state" (*Globe*, July 30): the truth that the preamble set the tone for the whole document.

This fact has been borne out in a few cases where judges have used the preamble to discern the founders' intent for other parts of the constitution. One 1959 case sought to stop a Spokane school district from allowing children to leave school for one hour of private religious instruction, arguing it was unconstitutional. The state Supreme Court disagreed, using the language in the preamble and other places to determine that "it was never the intention [of the founders] that our constitution should be construed in a manner indicating any hostility toward religion" (*Perry v. School District No. 81*). Another court similarly used the preamble's reference to God to find that a volunteer chaplaincy program in the Pierce County Sheriff's Office didn't violate the constitution (*Malyon v. Pierce County*).

In 1989, Supreme Court Justice Utter argued that the preamble wording "grateful to the Supreme Ruler of the Universe *for our liberties*" shows that the founders did not see the constitution as a source of individual rights, but merely as a declaration of the inherent natural and common law rights already possessed by individuals (italics added). Utter translated this intent to mean that state action is not required for protection of free speech, because government is not the source of the right (*Southcenter Joint Venture v. National Democratic Policy Committee*).

While birthing the preamble was a painful process for the constitutional delegates, the final wording set the tone for the entire document: "We the people" are the source of the authority behind government, our individual rights were in existence long before the constitution was written, and there is a place for gratefulness to God even in the middle of a business meeting.

Cases

Perry v. School District No. 81, 54 Wash.2d 886 (1959)
Southcenter Joint Venture v. National Democratic Policy Committee, 113 Wash.2d 413 (1989) (Utter, J., concurring)
Malyon v. Pierce County, 131 Wash.2d 779 (1997)

Other Sources

"Red Hot Debates and Windy Oratory Prevails Throughout the Sessions," *Tacoma Morning Globe*, July 30, 1889

"Still Fooling Away Time Without a Pretense of Work," *Tacoma Morning Globe*, August 1, 1889

The Journal of the Washington State Constitutional Convention: 1889, at 491–94 (Beverly Paulik Rosenow ed., 1999)

Article I, Section 1: Political power.

All political power is inherent in the people, and governments derive their just powers from the consent of the governed, and are established to protect and maintain individual rights.

Section 1 makes a foundational statement for the entire state constitution by declaring the source of power for the document. The people are the true sovereigns of the state, and government only has power by their consent. The constitutional writers likely drew inspiration from documents, such as the *Federalist Papers*, which call the people "the only legitimate fountain of power . . . it is from them that the constitutional charter . . . is derived." As one Washington Supreme Court justice put it, Section 1 is "the lens through which we view all other Article I rights" (*In re Recall of West*).

Per Section 1, the written constitution is a delegation of broad powers from the sovereigns (the people) to a carefully constructed institution of government. This delegated power allows the state government to enact and enforce laws that "promote the health, peace, safety, and general welfare of the people of Washington," generally known as police powers (*State v. Crediford*).

This was not a delegation without purpose, however. Section 1 clearly lays out the goal: "to protect and maintain individual rights," echoing the Declaration of Independence, which states that governments are instituted to secure "certain unalienable rights," among which are "Life, Liberty, and the pursuit of Happiness." The authority granted by Washington's constitution is not a blank check the state government can use unreasonably to burden individual liberties. Thus, the rest of Article I and other sections of the constitution act as a check on the state's powers.

Section 1 was adopted with little fuss by the constitutional convention. The first draft was longer, incorporating more descriptive language about individual rights and the power of the people. The Bill of Rights Committee cut it down to the present size, except their version read, "all political power abides with the people." Republican Edward Eldridge from Whatcom successfully moved to substitute "all political power is inherent in the people" (*Journal*).

Though the adoption was relatively smooth, however, the interpretation of this section has caused some wrangling in the courts. For example, in 1935, the Supreme Court said, "Under our form of government, ultimate sovereignty, so far as the state is concerned, rests in its people, and so long as the government established by them exists, that sovereignty remains with them" (*Love v. King County*). But in 1968, the court restated its view, saying, "So far as the power of the legislature is not limited by the constitution, it is unrestrained" (*In re Elliott*). And in a 2007 decision, one justice took issue with the broad deference the Supreme Court majority gave to the legislature, arguing, "[Section 1] hardly evidences our state government has the inherent power to do anything. Rather, it stands for precisely the opposite" (*Washington State Farm Bureau v. Gregoire*).

Thomas Cooley, the leading constitutional law scholar at the time of the Washington convention, explains some of the intent behind provisions like Section 1, "The will of the people, as declared in the Constitution, is the final law; and the will of the legislature is law only when it is in harmony with, or at least not opposed to, that controlling instrument." The legislature generally represents the interests of the people in the day-to-day business of government, but it cannot write valid laws that infringe on individual rights.

Through the years, some have argued that Section 1 contains an implicit power of initiative or referendum, but the courts have not agreed, pointing to Article II, Section 1 as the only constitutional basis for those rights.

Cases

State v. Clark, 30 Wash 439 (1902)

Love v. King County, 181 Wash. 462 (1935)

In re Elliott, 74 Wash.2d 600, 604 (1968)

CLEAN v. State, 130 Wash.2d 782 (1996)

State v. Crediford, 130 Wash.2d 747, 751-752 (1996)

Philadelphia II v. Gregoire, 128 Wash.2d 707, 718 (1996)

State v. Matthews, 93 Wash.App. 1090 (1999)

In re Recall of West, 155 Wash.2d 659, 669 (2005) (J. Johnson, J., concurring)

Washington State Farm Bureau v. Gregoire, 162 Wash.2d 284 (2007) (Sanders, J., concurring)

Other Sources

Thomas M. Cooley, *Treatise on the Constitutional Limitations,* at 5 (5th ed. 1883)

The Journal of the Washington State Constitutional Convention: 1889, at 494–95 (Beverly Paulik Rosenow ed., 1999)

Article I, Section 2: Supreme law of the land.

The Constitution of the United States is the supreme law of the land.

When conflicts occur between national and state governments, Article VI, Section 2 of the U.S. Constitution has declared the federal Constitution to be supreme. Decisions of the U.S. Supreme Court interpreting the Constitution are final and binding, and the Washington Constitution explicitly recognizes this supremacy.

The Supremacy Clause is not all-encompassing, however. The federal government is one of limited, enumerated powers granted by the Constitution, and the powers not delegated to it are reserved to the states. As James Madison wrote in the *Federalist Papers*: "The powers delegated by the proposed Constitution to the Federal Government, are few and defined. Those which are to remain in the State Governments are numerous and indefinite."

Just one year after Washington was granted statehood, the Supreme Court of Washington observed that "section 2 only relates to those matters wherein the general government assumes to control the individual states," and the provision "was not intended to carry the principle further than this in our constitution" (*In re Rafferty*).

Additionally, the U.S. Supreme Court has recognized that each state has the "sovereign right to adopt in its own Constitution individual liberties more expansive than those conferred by the Federal Constitution" (*Pruneyard Shopping Center v. Robins*). When presented with parallel provisions, Washington courts rely on several factors to determine whether the Washington Constitution extends broader rights to its citizens than the U.S. Constitution: textual language, differences in the texts, constitutional history, preexisting state law, structural differences, and matters of particular state or local concern.

Section 2 was adopted by the constitutional convention with very little debate. Similar clauses are found in the constitutions of many of Washington's statehood contemporaries, including Idaho, North Dakota, South Dakota, and Wyoming.

Cases

In re Rafferty, 1 Wash. 382 (1890)
Moen v. Erlandson, 80 Wash.2d 755 (1972)
Pruneyard Shopping Center v. Robins, 447 U.S. 74 (1980)
State v. Gunwall, 106 Wash.2d 54 (1986)

Other Sources

James Madison, *The Federalist Papers*, No. 45 (1788)
Index Digest of State Constitutions, Columbia University (2nd ed., Oceana Press Inc., 1959)
The Journal of the Washington State Constitutional Convention: 1889, at 495 (Beverly Paulik Rosenow ed., 1999)

Article I, Section 3: Personal rights.

No person shall be deprived of life, liberty, or property, without due process of law.

✤ ✤ ✤

"Due process" is an ancient and often difficult to understand legal term of art, yet it is a foundational protection for individual liberties. The inclusion of this clause was not a novel move by the writers of the Washington Constitution, as it can be found in almost identical fashion in the U.S. Constitution and at least twenty-five other state constitutions.

The origins of due process stretch back through the English common law all the way to the Magna Carta (1215). It has always meant that the general law of the land is to protect every person's life, liberty, and property. Conversely, its application is usually to restrain the passage or application of laws that take away one of these rights. Applying due process is intensely factual, since whether a person has been afforded due process entirely depends on his or her respective situation. What may be adequate due process in one case may not be in another.

Both federal and Washington state courts have broken down the due process requirement of Section 3 into two parts: procedural due process and substantive due process. In both types, the protections of due process apply only if a government entity or official is involved.

The heart of **procedural due process** is ensuring that a person gets his or her day in court. Any time one's life, liberty, or property is burdened by government action, an opportunity must be provided for a fair hearing. That hearing must include

(1) clear notice to the individual of the hearing, (2) an opportunity to be heard before a competent judge in an orderly proceeding, (3) the opportunity to know the claims of the opposing parties, and (4) reasonable preparation time before the hearing (*Cuddy v. State*).

Substantive due process prevents the state from abusing its "police powers" to arbitrarily impair one's life, liberty, or property. The key word is "arbitrary," since a state does have the responsibility for keeping its populace safe and healthy, and doing so will often necessitate some kind of burden on individual rights. But if an action burdens an element of life, liberty, or property rights, such as the free exercise of religion or speech, a state must prove that its action is not arbitrary, but based on a compelling interest, such as a major threat to public health, peace, or safety. The state must also show there is no easier way to satisfy its compelling interest. A court will balance that interest against the burden on the individual's fundamental rights. It's very difficult for a state to meet this high standard.

Because Washington's due process provision is nearly identical to that in the federal Constitution, federal case law has been given great weight in Washington cases. Several times the state Supreme Court has found no difference between the due process protections offered by the federal or state constitutions.

Despite the similarities in constitutional text, however, Washington courts have deviated from federal court decisions in one area: property rights. Federal courts have largely abandoned the use of due process in property litigation, focusing instead on the "takings" clause (U.S. Constitution, Amendment V). But Washington courts have continued to review property cases under the substantive due process test. This affords greater protection to Washington citizens, because a due process violation can invalidate a law, whereas a takings violation can only result in compensation of the harmed individual. (See Article I, Section 16 for more information on takings.)

Therefore, to justify under Section 3 a law burdening or taking private property, the state must show that the law (1) achieves a legitimate public purpose, (2) the elements in the law are reasonably necessary to fulfill that purpose, and (3) the law is not unduly oppressive on individuals. Without this kind of compelling interest and reasonable enforcement, a law will be struck down as violating substantive due process (*Rivett v. City of Tacoma*).

Besides property regulations, Washington courts have also slightly deviated from federal decisions to give greater protection for the free exercise of religion and for criminal defendants in death penalty cases.

Cases

State v. Seattle Taxicab & Transfer Co., 90 Wash. 416 (1916)

Cuddy v. State, Dept. of Public Assistance, 74 Wash.2d (1968)

Olympic Forest Products, Inc. v. Chaussee Corp., 82 Wash.2d 418 (1973)

Young v. Konz, 91 Wash.2d 532 (1979)

State v. Bartholomew, 101 Wash.2d 631 (1984)

State v. McCullough, 56 Wash.App. 655 (1990)

State v. Ortiz, 119 Wash.2d 294 (1992)

Rivett v. City of Tacoma, 123 Wash.2d 573 (1994)

Munns v. Martin, 131 Wash.2d 192 (1997)

Other Sources

The Journal of the Washington State Constitutional Convention: 1889, at 495–96 (Beverly Paulik Rosenow ed., 1999)

Article I, Section 4:
Right of petition and assemblage.

The right of petition and of the people peaceably to assemble for the common good shall never be abridged.

✢ ✢ ✢

The right of citizens to petition their government can be traced back to the Magna Carta (1215) and the English Declaration of Rights (1689). Under this provision, people are guaranteed the right to "peaceably assemble and to make such recommendations as they may conclude are for the common good, and to petition all other citizens to join them" (*State v. Dykeman*). The right allows "uninhibited and open debate on public issues" (*State v. Gossett*).

Washington's petition and assembly clause differs slightly from the assembly clause in the First Amendment of the U.S. Constitution, raising the question of whether the state clause should be given a different meaning. Generally, differences in structure between federal and state constitutions favor an independent state interpretation. The Supreme Court of Washington considered this question in 1996 and chose to interpret Washington's right of petition equal to the First Amendment.

Section 4, however, is qualified by the phrase "for the common good," a phrase that appears in many other state constitutions. A motion to strike this phrase failed at the constitutional convention.

The facts in *Richmond v. Thompson* illustrate how the "common good" phrase qualifies the right of petition. After receiving a speeding citation, a citizen contacted the Office of the Gov-

ernor, alleging the trooper had assaulted him and threatened to
"blow my brains out." An investigation cleared the trooper of
any wrongdoing, and the trooper sued the citizen for defamation. The citizen argued his statements were protected by Section 4. The Supreme Court of Washington ruled the right of
petition is not absolute, and recklessly made false statements are
not in the "common good."

The right of assembly may also be subject to "reasonable
restraints," as an appeals court said in *State v. Gossett.* This case
involved a student who trespassed on a construction site with approximately fifty demonstrators to protest racial discrimination
in the construction trades. The court ruled that if an assembly
violates the rights of others or injures property, "the government
may curtail the time, place and manner of assembly or speech in
order that liberty not become license."

One of the relevant "time, place, manner" questions is *where*
citizens may lawfully gather, as the right to assemble does not
extend to all locations. The court in *Gossett* ruled that citizens
might assemble on public property in common use by the public, so long as the assembly does not interfere with the conduct
of others. The use of public property not generally open to the
public may be restrained. Additionally, ordinances that facilitate
the movement of traffic do not unconstitutionally abridge the
right to assemble. Instead, such laws are a reasonable exercise
of police power. For example, in *City of Tacoma v. Roe*, protesters
ordered to move after blocking pedestrian traffic on a sidewalk
were not unconstitutionally deprived of their right to assemble.

Washington courts have ruled that Section 4 grants a right
of *political* petition and does not involve an unlimited right of access to the courts. Sections 9, 10, 21, and 22 of Article I address
citizens' rights of access to court.

✤ ✤ ✤

Cases

State v. Dykeman, 70 Wash. 599 (1912)
City of Tacoma v. Roe, 190 Wash. 444 (1937)
State v. Gossett, 11 Wash.App. 864 (1974)
Housing Authority of King County v. Saylors, 87 Wash.2d 732 (1977)
Richmond v. Thompson, 130 Wash.2d 368 (1996)

Other Sources

The Journal of the Washington State Constitutional Convention: 1889, at 496 (Beverly Paulik Rosenow ed., 1999)
Robert F. Utter & Hugh D. Spitzer, *The Washington State Constitution: A Reference Guide,* at 19 (2002)

Article I, Section 5: Freedom of speech

Every person may freely speak, write and publish on all subjects, being responsible for the abuse of that right.

✤ ✤ ✤

Freedom of speech has been called "a keystone right enabling us to preserve all other rights," and "the Constitution's most majestic guarantee" (*Nelson v. McClatchy Newspapers*). With a few exceptions, this section protects the right of all Washington residents to speak, write, and publish at will and prevents government from enacting laws restricting these activities.

In 1898 the Washington Supreme Court described a likely motivation behind including Section 5 in the constitution. Pointing out similar provisions in the federal and all other state constitutions, the justices said a common purpose was to prevent government from censoring "articles intended for publication." They decried this arbitrary practice, which existed in England before the American Revolution and was one of the motivations for the break from the mother country. According to the justices, such "censorship was inconsistent with free institutions" (*State v. Tugwell*).

Applying Section 5 requires answering three questions: (1) what kind of speech and writing is protected, (2) who is it protected from, and (3) how is it protected?

Freedom of speech is a frequently litigated constitutional right with many nuances, but in general it protects all types of speech and expression, especially noncommercial. It doesn't, however, act as a license for people to "advocate disregard for the law," for obscene speech, or for threatening military security

(*State v. Fox*). Nor does it provide immunity to lawsuits for libel or slander, as expressly stated in the latter half of Section 5: "being responsible for the abuse of that right."

In determining whether Section 5 is intended to protect against government, private parties, or both, it's important to note that the wording differs from the U.S. First Amendment, which says, "Congress shall make no law . . . abridging the freedom of speech. . . ." This wording makes it obvious the section is aimed at government actions, not private parties. Section 5 does not include this kind of limiting statement, making the scope of protection unclear and the subject of much debate.

The state Supreme Court struggled with this question in several cases involving restrictions imposed by private corporations, such as malls and grocery stores, on activities such as protesting or signature-gathering. The court first determined that Section 5 did apply to private parties, but departed from that interpretation in later cases. Currently the courts seem to have settled on the view that because the Washington Constitution acts as a limit on *state* power, Section 5 is only applicable to government actions, providing no protection against private parties (with exceptions for initiative or referendum circulation, based on Article II, Section 1).

In both federal and Washington courts, a distinction is made, based on where the speech takes place, or its "forum." In public forums, such as parks and public squares, speech is fully protected. In non-public forums, such as government office buildings, speech receives less protection. Commercial speech, such as billboards and advertisements, also receives less protection.

Can government restrict speech, even in a public forum? Yes, but only within a very narrow category. A law can regulate the time, place, or manner of the speech, but not the speech content. The government must show that it has a compelling (i.e., very strong) interest in the purpose of the law, there is no easier way to achieve its purpose, and there are alternative ways available for people to speak.

For example, the Supreme Court struck down a public-housing facility rule that banned signs on residents' doors, holding that there were less restrictive ways to achieve the facility's aesthetic goals and that door signs were a unique form of communication not replaceable by available alternatives. However, the Supreme Court upheld a library's policy of filtering Internet content deemed harmful to minors, concluding that libraries are permitted to exercise discretion in literary acquisitions and this discretion should extend to websites.

Early Washington cases on Section 5 focused on the constitutionality of newspaper articles' inciting civil disobedience or disparaging court decisions. Since then, the development of balancing tests for Section 5 has closely tracked federal decisions. In some cases, Section 5 gives greater protection to speech than the First Amendment. For example, the First Amendment requires states to only show a *significant* interest in the purpose of a law restricting speech, a lower standard than Washington's requirement for *compelling* interest. Additionally, the state constitution prohibits prior restraints on speech.

Cases

State v. Tugwell, 19 Wash. 238 (1898)
State v. Fox, 71 Wash. 185 (1912)
State v. Hazeltine, 82 Wash. 81 (1914)
State v. Haffer, 94 Wash. 136 (1916)

State v. Wilson, 137 Wash 125 (1925)

Alderwood Assocs. v. Washington Envtl. Coun., 96 Wash.2d 230, 245 (1981)

State v. Coe, 101 Wash.2d 364 (1984)

Bering v. SHARE, 106 Wash.2d 212 (1986)

Southcenter Joint Venture v. National Democratic Policy Committee, 113 Wash.2d 413 (1989)

National Federation of Retired Persons v. Insurance Commissioner, 120 Wash.2d 101 (1992)

Ino Ino, Inc. v. City of Bellevue, 132 Wash.2d 103 (1997)

Nelson v. McClatchy Newspapers, 131 Wash.2d 523 (1997)

Waremart, Inc. v. Progressive Campaigns, Inc., 139 Wash.2d 623 (1999)

Resident Action Council v. Seattle Housing Authority, 162 Wash.2d 773 (2008)

Bradburn v. North Cent. Regional Library Dist., 168 Wash.2d 789 (2010)

Other Sources

U.S. Constitution, Amendment 1

Article I, Section 6:
Oaths – mode of administering.

The mode of administering an oath, or affirmation, shall be such as may be most consistent with and binding upon the conscience of the person to whom such oath, or affirmation, may be administered.

✠ ✠ ✠

This provision allows those who take an oath (or affirmation) to do so in a manner consistent with their own conscience. Washington's language is modeled on constitutional provisions in Indiana (Art. I § 8) and Oregon (Art. I § 7). Similarly, the U.S. Constitution (Art. II § 1) allows the President to take an oath of office by swearing or affirming.

Indiana's oath provision has been attributed to the state's wide array of religious beliefs and practices, which included Methodist, Baptist, Presbyterian, Roman Catholic, Quaker, Lutheran, Jewish, United Brethren, and Disciples of Christ, as well as those unaffiliated with any religious congregation. The Indiana delegates' respect for this variety led them to allow flexibility in the oath-taking procedure when adopting the 1851 Indiana Constitution.

Washington courts have said that Section 6 provides "wide discretion" as to the mode of administering an oath (*State v. Collier*). The goal of any procedure is to employ a mode that will be most binding upon the person. Accordingly, a trial judge's request that an eight-year-old witness "promise" to tell the truth was acceptable, as "promise" would be more comprehensible than "swear" for a child.

✠ ✠ ✠

Cases

State v. Collier, 23 Wash.2d 678 (1945)

Schoultz v. Department of Motor Vehicles, 89 Wash.2d 664 (1977)

City Chapel Evangelical Free Inc. v. City of South Bend, 744 N.E.2d 443 (2001)

Article I, Section 7:
Invasion of private affairs or home prohibited.

No person shall be disturbed in his private affairs or his home invaded, without authority of law.

✤ ✤ ✤

An oft-used and incredibly important protection for individual liberty, Section 7 prevents the government from invading a person's home, person, or privacy. The only time such an invasion is allowed is if a judge specifically orders it in a subpoena or warrant, which can only happen in a very limited set of circumstances.

Section 7 is analogous to the Fourth Amendment to the U.S. Constitution, which reads:

> The right of the people to be secure in their persons, houses, papers, and effects, against unreasonable searches and seizures, shall not be violated, and no warrants shall issue, but upon probable cause, supported by oath or affirmation, and particularly describing the place to be searched, and the person or things to be seized.

Known as the "search and seizure" clause, a quick glance shows the wording is very different from Section 7. The first draft by the Washington constitutional convention was more like the Fourth Amendment, but the Bill of Rights Committee decided to alter the language drastically in the final text. The committee members may have been influenced by an 1886 case in which the U.S. Supreme Court strongly affirmed individuals' rights against unlawful government invasions into "personal security, personal liberty, and private property" (*Origin and Development of Washington's Exclusionary Rule*). Using language from this case demonstrated the commitment of the constitutional writers to a straightforward and unambiguous protection of an individual's rights.

Despite the marked difference in language, early court cases tracked closely with federal decisions, especially after 1961, when the U.S. Supreme Court determined that the Fourth Amendment applied to states.

This trend started to reverse in the 1978 case of *State v. Hehman*, when the state Supreme Court said Section 7 prohibited a police officer from arresting a person who had committed minor traffic violations and had promised to appear in court. Prior federal court decisions had found such an arrest allowable under the Fourth Amendment.

In 1984, the state Supreme Court continued this independent trend by parting with the federal courts in the test used to determine if an arrest or search warrant is valid. Several more departures from federal decisions culminated in the 1984 case of *State v. Myrick*, in which the state Supreme Court declared that "the unique language of [Section 7] provides greater protection to persons under the Washington constitution than [the Fourth Amendment] provides to persons generally." The Fourth Amendment asks only if a person has a "reasonable expectation of privacy," an answer that will differ as technology and customs change. But Section 7 protects a person's "private affairs": those things people traditionally have believed should be private.

For example, the court found Section 7 to prohibit an unwarranted search of a person's garbage cans, even though garbage is not protected by the Fourth Amendment. Similarly, Section 7 protects against government invasion into bank and telephone records, and against unwarranted searches of cars, even when driven by a felon on work release. But a warrant is not required to search drivers' license records.

Unfortunately, this "private affairs" standard as declared in *Myrick* is somewhat vague, causing confusion among the lower courts in subsequent decades. Some judges even decided to apply all or part of the federal test in contradiction to *Myrick*. But the state Supreme Court held firm to its separate state constitutional analysis. In the 2007 case of *State v. Miles*, the justices reiterated that Section 7 has its own two-part analysis: (1) whether the incident in question is a governmental intrusion into a person's private affairs, and, if so, (2) whether "authority of law" justified the intrusion. As mentioned above, authority of law usually refers to a warrant or order issued by a judge. There are a few situations in which a warrantless government invasion or arrest is allowed, such as when there is danger to police officers or when there is risk evidence will be destroyed. But the prosecutor must prove these exceptions.

In 2009, the U.S. Supreme Court modified its rule about warrantless vehicle searches in *Arizona v. Gant*. The court held that police may only search a vehicle incident to an arrest if it is reasonable to believe that the arrestee might access the vehicle at the time of the arrest, or that the vehicle contains evidence related to the arrest. This decision led to a number of decisions by the Washington State Supreme Court that adopted and even strengthened the *Gant* rule. For example, a warrantless search was not permitted where the police attempted an arrest of a person who stood next to his vehicle (*State v. Patton*); a warrantless search of a vehicle is not justified solely on the believe that the vehicle contains evidence of the crime unless the search is necessary to prevent destruction or concealment of the evidence (*State v. Valdez*); and the police could not conduct a warrantless search of a vehicle simply because a vehicle's passenger had an outstanding warrant for the crime of trespass (*State v. Afana*).

In sum, Section 7 is unusual among Article I provisions, in that it has a fully developed line of cases based entirely upon state constitutional grounds, and these cases grant individuals greater protection than the federal counterpart.

Cases

State v. Hehman, 90 Wash.2d 45 (1978)

State v. Houser, 95 Wash.2d 143 (1980)

State v. Myrick, 102 Wash.2d 506 (1984)

State v. Gunwall, 106 Wash.2d 54 (1986)

State v. Berber, 48 Wash.App. 583 (1987)

State v. Boland, 115 Wash.2d 571 (1990)

State v. Hendrickson, 129 Wash.2d 61 (1996)

State v. McKinney, 148 Wash.2d 20 (2002)

State v. Miles, 160 Wash.2d 236 (2007)

Arizona v. Gant, 129 S.Ct. 1710 (2009)

State v. Patton, 167 Wash.2d 379 (2009)

State v. Valdez, 167 Wash.2d. 761 (2009)

State v. Afana, 169 Wash.2d 169 (2010)

Other Sources

U.S. Constitution, Amendment 4

The Journal of the Washington State Constitutional Convention: 1889, at 497 (Beverly Paulik Rosenow ed., 1999)

Sanford E. Pitler, *The Origin and Development of Washington's Independent Exclusionary Rule: Constitutional Right and Constitutionally Compelled Remedy*, 61 Wash. L. Rev. 459, 519–21 (1986)

Article I, Section 8: Irrevocable privilege, franchise or immunity prohibited.

No law granting irrevocably any privilege, franchise or immunity, shall be passed by the legislature.

✢ ✢ ✢

Constitutional scholar Thomas Cooley notes the reasons for prohibiting irrevocable or perpetual laws.

> To say that the legislature may pass irrepealable laws is to say that it may alter the very constitution from which it derives its authority; since, insofar as one legislature could bind a subsequent one by its enactments, it could in the same degree reduce the legislative power of its successors; and the process might be repeated, until, one by one, the subjects of legislation would be excluded altogether from their control, and the constitutional provision that the legislative power shall be vested in two houses would be to a greater or less degree rendered ineffectual.

A franchise is the right granted by the state or a municipality to an existing corporation or to an individual to do certain things which that the corporation or individual otherwise cannot do. For example, "the right to use a street or alley for a commercial or street railroad track, or to erect thereon poles and string wires for telegraph, telephone, or electric light purposes, or to use the street or alley underneath the surface for water pipes, gas pipes, or other conduits" (*Washington Water Power Co. v. Rooney*).

The Washington Supreme Court ruled in 1931 that a statute regulating automobile transportation companies and requiring certificates of convenience on state public highways, which are subject to states' control, was not an irrevocable grant, privilege, or franchise in violation of this constitutional provision.

A 1968 Attorney General Opinion stated that a third-class city was not authorized to enact an ordinance granting a perpetual franchise to a railroad company to permit the railroad to lay its tracks and spur lines across city streets and rights-of-way and to operate its trains across said tracks and spur lines. The opinion noted a similar provision in the Alabama Constitution. Interpreting the provision, the Alabama Supreme Court observed in 1885: "Free competition in all departments of commercial traffic is justly deemed to be the life of a people's prosperity. The policy of the law, as now declared by our constitution, is as clear in the condemnation of the grant of irrevocable exclusive privileges conferred by franchise, as that of the common law was in the reprobation of pure monopolies. . . ." (*Birmingham & Pratt Mines v. Birmingham Street Ry. Co.*).

Cases

Birmingham & Pratt Mines v. Birmingham Street Ry. Co., 79 Ala. 465 (1885)

State v. Inland Forwarding Corp., 164 Wash. 412 (1931)

Washington Water Power Co. v. Rooney, 3 Wash.2d 642 (1940)

MAC Amusement Co. v. State Dept. of Revenue, 95 Wash.2d 963 (1981)

Other Sources

Thomas M. Cooley, *Treatise on the Constitutional Limitations*, at
    246 (8th ed. 1927)
Washington Attorney General Opinion, No. 32 (1968)

Article I, Section 9: Rights of accused persons.

No person shall be compelled in any criminal case to give evidence against himself, or be twice put in jeopardy for the same offense.

✚ ✚ ✚

It was "a universal maxim of the common law of England, that no man is to be brought in jeopardy more than once for the same offence." Thus Sir William Blackstone, the preeminent legal scholar at the time of America's founding, described the long tradition behind part two of Section 9, known as the "double-jeopardy" clause. The first part is no less noteworthy, having its roots in abuses by the English courts long before the Revolutionary War.

In fact, that historical tradition probably led to the inclusion of Section 9 in the Washington Constitution. The state Supreme Court speculated in a 1945 case that "candidly speaking . . . it is more likely that the provision [Section 9] was inserted in Article I, entitled 'Bill of Rights,' because it was in the Federal bill of rights and had been included in the constitutions of practically all of the states that had theretofore entered the Union" (*State v. Brunn*). The writers of Section 9 likely patterned it after the Oregon Constitution and the Fifth Amendment of the U.S. Constitution.

Self-Incrimination Clause

The primary difference between the Fifth Amendment ("nor shall be compelled in any criminal case to be a witness against himself") and Section 9 is the substitution of the word "evidence" for "witness." In at least one case, a defendant argued this difference was meaningful, but the state Supreme Court determined that Section 9's wording "envisions the same guarantee as that provided in the federal constitution" (*State v. Moore*). Washington state courts have consistently interpreted both the federal and state guarantees against self-incrimination as equal.

To invoke the right against self-incrimination, one must show two things: (1) the testimony is compulsory, and (2) the testimony involves "evidence."

A person voluntarily testifying against himself cannot claim the right; it must be involuntary testimony. And by "involuntary," the section doesn't refer only to being stretched on a rack or other types of torture (although that has been a problem at times in English history). In our day, it usually takes the form of a person being faced with a "no-win" situation, in that if they testify truthfully, they incriminate themselves; and if they testify falsely, they commit perjury; and if they refuse to testify, they are held in contempt of court, or their denial is used to show guilt. Such a "cruel trilemma" is prohibited under Section 9 (*City of Seattle v. Stalsbroten*).

There are two primary stages when a person can claim the privilege: upon arrest and at trial. Washington courts follow the famous federal case of *Miranda v. Arizona*, requiring that upon arrest a person must be informed of his or her right "to remain silent." At trial, a defendant cannot be forced to testify, and a prosecutor cannot directly or indirectly infer guilt because of this refusal.

Many Washington cases have reviewed what "evidence" means, often in cases involving arrests for drunk driving under the state's "Implied Consent" law. According to this law, people who drive on Washington roads are deemed to have given consent for a breath or blood test to determine alcohol content. In 1971, the state Supreme Court reviewed the constitutionality of this law under Section 9 and upheld it in part because breath and blood samples are not "testimonial or communicative evidence." The decision was consistent with other state and federal cases holding that some actions are not covered under Section 9, such as removing clothing to show a tattoo, providing fingerprints, showing a drivers' license, providing handwriting samples, or participating in a police line-up.

Double-Jeopardy Clause

The second part of Section 9 protects individuals from being punished (put "in jeopardy") twice for the same action. For example, if a person shoots at someone and misses, they can't be charged with both assault and attempted murder.

As in the first part of Section 9, Washington courts have not found any substantive difference between this state constitutional right and the nearly identical federal protection in the Fifth Amendment. The biggest question in applying this right is what "same offense" means, although there has also been controversy in recent cases over whether a civil judgment (like repossession of property) counts as a punishment under Section 9.

An 1896 case established the test for "same offense" which Washington courts have followed in various forms ever since. That case dealt with the theft by fraud of a beaver shoulder cape, for which the thief was charged with two different crimes. The court didn't find double jeopardy, however, because the facts needed to prove one crime were not necessary for the other, and the elements of the two crimes were different. To find double jeopardy "the offenses must be identical both in fact and in law" (*State v. Reiff*). This came to be known as the "same elements" test, and is identical to the federal test (the *Blockburger* test). Because Washington courts track so closely on this issue with federal courts, there was a brief hiccup in 1990 when the U.S. Supreme Court added a new requirement to the same elements test. Washington courts did not embrace the change, however, and the U.S. Supreme Court reversed itself three years later.

Another shift occurred in 1994, when the U.S. Supreme Court indicated that a civil forfeiture of property, like repossession of a car, could be considered a "punishment." If someone were punished in a civil case, it would violate the double jeopardy prohibition to punish them also with a criminal sentence. Washington courts started to follow this interpretation, but reversed course in a 5-4 decision three years later when the U.S. Supreme Court changed its mind. The dissent complained that this about-face made it appear that the court was "allowing federal precedent to rewrite our state constitution" (*State v. Catlett*).

More recently, the Washington Supreme Court stated that sentencing enhancements, such as allowing harsher punishment when a firearm is used in the commission of a crime, do not violate double jeopardy.

Cases

State v. Reiff, 14 Wash. 664 (1896)
State v. Brunn, 22 Wash.2d 120 (1945)
Miranda v. Arizona, 384 U.S. 436 (1966)
State v. West, 70 Wash.2d 751 (1967)
State v. Moore, 79 Wash.2d 51 (1971)
State v. Clark, 124 Wash.2d 90 (1994)
State v. Gocken, 127 Wash.2d 95 (1995)
State v. Easter, 130 Wash.2d 228 (1996)
State v. Catlett, 133 Wash.2d 355 (1997)

City of Seattle v. Stalsbroten, 138 Wash.2d 227 (1999)
State v. Templeton, 148 Wash.2d 193 (2002)
In re Orange, 152 Wash.2d 795 (2004)
State v. Kelley, 168 Wash.2d 72 (2010)

Other Sources

Robert F. Utter & Hugh D. Spitzer, *The Washington State Constitution: A Reference Guide,* at 23 (2002)

Article I, Section 10: Administration of justice.

Justice in all cases shall be administered openly, and without unnecessary delay.

✦ ✦ ✦

The origins of Washington's open justice provision can be traced through American jurisprudence and centuries of English common law. The importance of public justice has long been recognized. As U.S. Supreme Court Chief Justice Warren Burger wrote in *Richmond Newspapers v. Virginia*, "People in an open society do not demand infallibility from their institutions, but it is difficult for them to accept what they are prohibited from observing."

Reviewing open court practices throughout history, Chief Justice Burger noted that cases in England were attended by the freemen of the community even before the Norman Conquest. "Somewhat like modern jury duty, attendance at these early meetings was compulsory on the part of the freemen, who were called upon to render judgment." Eventually, the duty to attend trials was relaxed, but trials remained public. Sir Edward Coke discussed the phrase *in curia domini regis* ("in the king's court") in his commentary on the Statute of Marlborough, passed by King Henry III in 1267: "These words are of great importance, for all Causes ought to be heard, ordered, and determined before the Judges of the King's Courts openly in the King's Courts, wither all persons may resort. . . . " Other English common law jurists wrote of the importance of openness in judicial administration (Sir Thomas Smith, 1513–77; Matthew Hale, 1609–76; William Blackstone, 1723–80).

The system of open justice was included in early American legal documents. The 1677 New Jersey Constitution provided that any person could attend civil or criminal trials. The 1682 Pennsylvania Constitution, drafted by William Penn, provided that "all courts shall be open," as did the 1776 Pennsylvania Constitution. The Sixth Amendment of the U.S. Constitution guarantees that in all criminal prosecutions, "the accused shall enjoy the right to a speedy and public trial."

So it is no surprise this legal tradition is clearly spelled out in Washington's state constitution. Section 10 guarantees the *public's* right to open and accessible court proceedings. "The open operation of our courts is of utmost public importance. Justice must be conducted openly to foster the public's understanding and trust in our judicial system and to give judges the check of public scrutiny" (*Dreiling v. Jain*).

The open administration of justice includes the right of media to observe and report on judicial proceedings. Accordingly, Washington court rules permit video and audio recording by news media at the judge's discretion.

The right of public access generally extends to jury selection in criminal cases, pretrial hearings, trials and exhibits, transcripts, and previously sealed discovery documents. A statute that sealed the identity of child victims of sexual assault was ruled unconstitutional, as it failed to address closure on a case-by-case basis.

Court decisions have limited when Section 10 would apply. The provision, for example, did not give an attorney the right to review a judge's personal computer files made for the judge's use in deciding cases. The section applies only to court proceedings, and not to administrative hearings such as a public university's disciplinary proceeding against a professor. Additionally, Section 10 does not grant access to a search warrant affidavit until charges relating to the investigation involving the affidavit are filed. "Closures" in which a disruptive spectator is excluded from the courtroom or seating is limited in the courtroom do not violate the public trial requirement.

Section 10 was viewed as mandatory from the earliest cases interpreting the provision, as early as 1897. The public's right to open proceedings, however, is not absolute, and may be limited to protect other interests at stake. For example, exclusion of the press from a pretrial hearing was justified to protect a defendant's right to a fair trial.

Given the "high order of constitutional protection of public's right to open proceedings," closure is to occur only in "rare circumstances" (*State v. Bone-Club*). Trial courts must conduct a case-by-case analysis to determine if closure is appropriate, evaluating five criteria. First, the advocate of closure must show there is a "serious and imminent threat" to an important interest; second, an opportunity to object must be provided to those present; third, the court should analyze whether the method for curtailing access is the least restrictive means available and effective in protecting the interests threatened; fourth, the court must weigh competing interests of the proponent of closure and the public; and fifth, closure must be no broader than necessary to serve its purpose (*Seattle Times Co. v. Ishikawa*).

Failure of a court to give a public trial or to follow the five-step closure test violates the right to public trial, and a new trial is required.

As Article I, Section 22 specifically grants defendants the right to a "speedy public trial," there is some question of whether a defendant can waive the open trial right. Section 10, however, is a right held by the *public*, separate from the individual defendant's right, and an individual cannot waive the public's right to open proceedings. A defendant can request closure, but this will be granted only if justified by the five-point analysis.

Cases

Rauch v. Chapman, 16 Wash. 568 (1897)

State v. Marsh, 126 Wash. 142 (1923)

Cohen v. Everett City Council, 85 Wash.2d 385 (1975)

Gannett Co. v. DePasquale, 443 U.S. 368 (1979)

Richmond Newspapers, Inc. v. Virginia, 448 U.S. 555 (1980)

Federated Publications, Inc. v. Kurtz, 94 Wash.2d 51 (1980)

Seattle Times Co. v. Ishikawa, 97 Wash.2d 30 (1982)

Seattle Times Co. v. Eberharter, 105 Wash.2d 144 (1986)

Allied Daily Newspapers v. Eikenberry, 121 Wash.2d 205 (1993)

State v. Bone-Club, 128 Wash.2d 254 (1995)

Beuhler v. Small, 115 Wash.App. 914 (2003)

Dreiling v. Jain, 151 Wash.2d 900 (2004)

In re Orange, 152 Wash.2d 795 (2004)

State v. Easterling, 157 Wash.2d 167 (2006)

State v. Momah, 141 Wash.App. 705 (2007)

State v. Duckett, 141 Wash.App. 797 (2007)

Mills v. Western Washington University, __ Wash.2d __ (2011)

Other Sources

Edward Coke, *Institutes of the Laws of England, Vol. II*, at 103 (6th ed. 1681)

Jonathan M. Hoffman, *By the course of the law: Origins of the open courts clause of state constitutions*, 74 Or.L.Rev. 1279 (1995)

Article I, Section 11: Religious freedom.

Absolute freedom of conscience in all matters of religious sentiment, belief and worship, shall be guaranteed to every individual, and no one shall be molested or disturbed in person or property on account of religion; but the liberty of conscience hereby secured shall not be so construed as to excuse acts of licentiousness or justify practices inconsistent with the peace and safety of the state. No public money or property shall be appropriated for or applied to any religious worship, exercise or instruction, or the support of any religious establishment: PROVIDED, HOWEVER, That this article shall not be so construed as to forbid the employment by the state of a chaplain for such of the state custodial, correctional, and mental institutions, or by a county's or public hospital district's hospital, health care facility, or hospice, as in the discretion of the legislature may seem justified. Nor religious qualification shall be required for any public office or employment, nor shall any person be incompetent as a witness or juror, in consequence of his opinion on matters of religion, nor be questioned in any court of justice touching his religious belief to affect the weight of his testimony.

Religious freedom has always been a fundamental tenet of the grand American experiment in democracy, but its focus has changed over the centuries. When our country's founding fathers broke away from England, their primary concern was to prevent the establishment of a national religion. That concern had faded by the time of the Washington constitutional convention, replaced with a new priority: religion in public education. Protestants had been the driving force behind the public education movement, which prompted Catholics to found many new parochial schools, raising the question of whether government funds could be channeled to those schools.

Attempts were made in 1875 and 1889 to amend the federal Constitution to include a prohibition against public money going to religious organizations. They failed, but Congress passed a law requiring new states to include this type of clause in their constitutions. As a consequence, three separate sections in Washington's state constitution restrict the use of public money for religious instruction: Article I, Section 11; Article IX, Section 4; and Article XXVI.

While the language on religious education is stricter than that of the federal Constitution, "Congress shall make no law respecting an establishment of religion, or prohibiting the free exercise thereof," the rest of Section 11 provides stronger protection to religious beliefs and practices, with phrases such as "absolute freedom of conscience." This language difference has played out in Washington courts, which have tended (especially in the past two decades) to give greater protection to religious freedoms than the federal courts.

Washington's constitutional delegates don't appear to have struggled in writing this section, although the final language differed substantially from the first draft, which was more like the U.S. First Amendment. Section 11 has been amended three times since passage—in 1904, 1958, and 1993—to add and expand upon the chaplaincy clause. This addition wouldn't likely have concerned the convention delegates, however, who as one of their first acts selected a chaplain and paid him (with public money) $1.50 per day to open each session with prayer.

Up through the mid-1980s, state courts consistently used federal interpretations of the U.S. First Amendment to settle religious liberty questions without really exploring the different language in the state constitution. The primary test used for determining whether a state action violated a person's right to exercise their religion freely came from a federal case, *Sherbert v. Verner* (1963). There, the U.S. Supreme Court said, "[A]ny incidental burden on the free exercise of appellant's religion may be justified (only) by a 'compelling state interest in the regulation of a subject within the State's constitutional power . . .'" (quoted in *City of Sumner v. First Baptist Church*). In other words, if a law places even a minor burden on a person's exercise of religion, the state must show that it has a very strong (compelling) public health or safety interest to justify the law, plus it must prove that there was no less-burdensome way to achieve the health or safety interest. If these tough requirements aren't met, the law is unconstitutional.

It was in the late 1980s when state courts first started to interpret Section 11 apart from the federal Constitution. In one major case, the state Supreme Court ruled it was a violation of the U.S. First Amendment to give financial aid to a blind student who was training to be a minister at a Bible college. The U.S. Supreme Court overturned the decision, ruling that the First Amendment did not prohibit such action. The case went back to the Washington Supreme Court, which found that the financial aid was unconstitutional under the *state constitution*, because the "sweeping and comprehensive language" of Section 11 "prohibits not only the *appropriation* of public money for religious instruction, but also the *application* of public funds to religious instruction" (emphasis in the original). The justices said that this was "a major difference between our state constitution and the . . . first amendment to the United States Constitution" (*Witters v. State of Washington Commission for the Blind*).

This development of a separate state interpretation accelerated after the U.S. Supreme Court's famous 1990 decision in *Employment Division v. Smith*, in which the court found that even if a law burdened religious beliefs, if it weren't specifically aimed at a religious practice and if it applied to the general population, it did not have to undergo the rigorous *Sherbert* "compelling interest" test. Washington Supreme Court justices responded negatively to this major shift, saying in a 1992 case, "[We] eschew the uncertainty of *Smith* II and rest our decision also on independent grounds under the Washington constitution. . . . The language of our state constitution is significantly different and stronger than the federal constitution" (*First Covenant Church v. City of Seattle*). Since then, state courts have continued to use the *Sherbert* test, based on the language of Section 11, to protect religious liberties.

Land use regulations on church-related property have fostered much Section 11 litigation in recent years. In some of these cases, the Supreme Court has started to pull back from the strong protections traditionally given to the free exercise of religion. The series began in 1982, when the court struck down the application of fire and safety codes to a church-operated school. It continued in 1992, when Seattle wanted to designate the buildings of First Covenant, a local church, as historical landmarks. Doing so would have made it difficult for the church to remodel its buildings, so the court ruled against Seattle, finding that landmark designation was not a compelling interest. A similar result was reached in several subsequent cases in the late 1990s, one of which strongly reiterated the Supreme Court's determination to not follow the federal *Smith* decision: "A facially neutral, even-handedly enforced statute that does not directly burden free exercise [of religion] may, nonetheless, violate Article I, Section 11, if it indirectly burdens the exercise of religion (*Munns v. Martin*).

But in 2000, the court veered away from this strict protection of religious liberties by declaring that zoning ordinances can trump the free exercise of religion. Clark County created a land-use plan that included no specific mention of churches, meaning that all churches had to apply for a special "conditional use" permit to operate. The eight-volume permit application cost more than $5,000 to file, with no guarantee it would be granted. Although the court found an incidental burden on the church they still upheld the zoning regulation, ruling, "We [the court] ought to require a very specific showing of hardship to justify exemption from land use restrictions" (*Open Door Baptist Church v. Clark County*). In 2009, the Supreme Court reached a result that was more accommodating to a church's application for a permit. The City of Woodinville had adopted a moratorium on temporary use permits and refused to process a temporary use permit from a church that sought to operate a homeless tent city on its property. The Supreme Court held the city had violated the church's exercise of religion, but stopped short of overruling *Open Door*.

State establishment of religion is a much less controversial part of Section 11, with state courts continuing to apply the federal test for such issues. That test comes from the 1971 case of *Lemon v. Kurtzman*, which requires laws to (1) have a secular purpose, (2) not have a primary effect of advancing religion, and (3) not excessively entangle church and state. One Washington case applying this test found that a chaplaincy program run by the Tacoma Police Department did not violate Section 11, since it had a secular purpose of crisis counseling, and any religious conversations that occurred were incidental.

✠ ✠ ✠

Cases

State v. Verbon, 167 Wash. 140 (1932)

Sherbert v. Verner, 374 U.S. 398 (1963)

Lemon v. Kurtzman, 403 U.S. 602 (1971)

City of Sumner v. First Baptist Church, 97 Wash.2d 1 (1982)

Witters v. State of Washington Commission for the Blind, 112 Wash.2d 363 (1986)

First Covenant Church v. City of Seattle, 120 Wash.2d 203 (1992)

First United Methodist Church v. Hearing Examiner, 129 Wash.2d 238 (1996)

Malyon v. Pierce County, 131 Wash.2d 779 (1997)

Munns v. Martin, 131 Wash.2d 192 (1997)

Open Door Baptist Church v. Clark County, 140 Wash.2d 143 (2000)

North Pacific Union Conference Ass'n of Seventh Day Adventists v. Clark County, 118 Wash.App. 22 (2003)

City of Woodinville v. Northshore United Church of Christ, 166 Wash.2d 633 (2009)

Other Sources

The Journal of the Washington State Constitutional Convention: 1889, at 7–9 (Beverly Paulik Rosenow ed., 1999)

Katie Hosford, *The search for a distinct religious-liberty jurisprudence under the Washington state constitution*, 75 Wash. L. Rev. 643 (2000)

Robert F. Utter & Hugh D. Spitzer, *The Washington State Constitution: A Reference Guide*, at 26 (2002)

Article I, Section 12:
Special privileges and immunities prohibited.

No law shall be passed granting to any citizen, class of citizens, or corporation other than municipal, privileges or immunities which upon the same terms shall not equally belong to all citizens, or corporations.

The privileges and immunities clause protects the "fundamental rights which belong to the citizens of the state by reason of such citizenship" (*State v. Vance*), including the right to carry on business, to acquire and hold property, to collect debts, to enforce other personal rights, and to be exempt from taxes or burdens from which citizens of some other state are exempt. An oft-cited description of these fundamental rights includes those that belong "to the citizens of all free governments; and which have, at all times, been enjoyed by the citizens of the several states which compose this Union, from the time of their becoming free, independent, and sovereign" (*Corfield v. Coryell*).

The phrase is rooted in history, is discussed by William Blackstone, appears in the Articles of Confederation (1778), is referred to by Alexander Hamilton in *Federalist* No. 80, and appears in the Virginia Declaration of Rights of 1776: "no man, or set of men, are entitled to exclusive or separate emoluments or privileges from the community. . . ." Eight of the other original colonies adopted similar provisions.

The Washington state privileges and immunities clause is modeled on the Oregon Constitution (Article I, Section 20), and courts have looked to the interpretation of Oregon's provision for guidance. The Oregon Supreme Court has stated: "The provisions of the state Constitution . . . prevent the enlargement of the rights of some in discrimination against the rights of others . . ." (*State v. Savage*).

Unlike Oregon, however, the Washington constitutional drafters added the word "corporation" to the privileges and immunities clause, as drafters hoped to prevent corporate manipulation of the lawmaking process. The question of limiting corporate power was one of the critical questions debated by the constitutional convention, and the framers tried to avoid placing such "burdensome restrictions in their constitution as would drive corporate enterprise out of the state" (Knapp, 239).

Historically, the Washington Supreme Court has viewed the state privileges and immunities clause and the federal equal protection clause as substantially identical. Equal protection generally requires that similarly situated persons be treated similarly under the law. In 1991, however, Justice Robert F. Utter wrote a concurring opinion in *Smith v. Smith* clarifying the distinctions between the two clauses. He noted that the emphasis is quite different:

> While both the Fourteenth Amendment and the state privileges and immunities clauses seek to prevent the State from distributing benefits and burdens unequally, they are focused on different concerns. The Fourteenth Amendment was enacted after the Civil War and its purpose was to eliminate the effects of slavery. It was intended to guarantee that certain classes of people (blacks) were not denied the benefits bestowed on other classes (whites), thereby granting equal treatment to all persons. Enacted after the Fourteenth Amendment, state privileges and immunities

clauses were intended to prevent people from
seeking certain privileges or benefits to the disad-
vantage of others. The concern was prevention of
favoritism and special treatment for a few, rather
than prevention of discrimination against dis-
favored individuals or groups.

The Supreme Court relied heavily on Justice Utter's opinion in 2004, when it ruled that the state privileges and immunities clause requires an analysis independent of the federal equal
protection clause. For a violation of Section 12 to occur, the law
(or its application) must confer a special privilege to certain
people or classes of citizens. The court must determine whether
the right at issue is fundamental, those rights belonging to the
citizens of the state by reason of their citizenship.

Numerous laws have been invalidated for granting privileges in the early twentieth century: a statute that exempted cereal
and flouring mills from certain "onerous" conditions imposed
on other corporations (*State v. Robinson Co.*); a city ordinance prohibiting the sale of fruits and vegetables within a city other than
farmers who grew produce themselves (*In re Application of Camp*);
a Spokane ordinance regulating employment agencies that imposed criminal penalties upon one party, but imposed no penalties for others in like circumstances (*City of Spokane v. Macho*);
and a Seattle ordinance that imposed a tax on sale of goods by
automatic devices that was not imposed upon merchants selling
the same class of goods (*City of Seattle v. Dencker*).

Other laws have been upheld despite Section 12 challenges:
a statute requiring a permit for pistol ownership (*State v. Tully*);
the petition method for property annexation (*Grant County*); the
state Defense of Marriage Act's prohibition against same-sex
marriage (*Andersen v. King County*); the state's disenfranchisement
scheme, which denies the right to vote to convicted felons who

have not completed all of the terms of their sentences, including full payment of their legal financial obligations (*Madison v. State*); a dissolution action, where one spouse had counsel while the other did not, was not a governmental grant of a special privilege to the represented spouse (*King v. King*); and a Seattle ordinance prohibiting solid waste hauling by all truckers except the city's contractors (*Ventenbergs*).

Equal Protection

Equal protection under the federal and state constitutions both require that persons similarly situated be similarly treated. When persons are not similarly treated, courts use a sliding scale to evaluate if an equal protection violation has occurred.

State action that threatens a fundamental right or affects a member of a "suspect class" (e.g., race, gender) must advance a compelling governmental interest using the least restrictive means possible. When "important" rights are threatened, the state action must be substantially related to an important government interest. When no suspect class or fundamental rights are threatened, the government action need only be rationally related to a legitimate government interest.

Cases

Corfield v. Coryell, 6 F. Cas. 546 (C.C.E.D.Pa.1823)
State v. Vance, 29 Wash. 435 (1902)
In re Application of Camp, 38 Wash. 393 (1905)
City of Spokane v. Macho, 51 Wash. 322 (1909)
City of Seattle v. Dencker, 58 Wash. 501 (1910)

State v. Robinson Co., 84 Wash. 246 (1915)

State v. Savage, 96 Or. 53 (1919)

State v. Tully, 198 Wash. 605 (1939)

State v. Smith, 117 Wash.2d 263 (1991)

State v. Shawn P., 122 Wash.2d 553 (1993)

Grant County Fire Protection Dist. No. 5 v. City of Moses Lake, 150 Wash.2d 791 (2004)

State v. Osman, 157 Wash.2d 474 (2006)

Andersen v. King County, 158 Wash.2d 1 (2006)

Madison v. State, 161 Wash.2d 85 (2007)

King v. King 162 Wash.2d 378 (2007)

Ventenbergs v. City of Seattle, 178 P.3d 960 (2008)

Other Sources

Lebbeus J. Knapp, *Origin of the Constitution of the State of Washington*, Washington Historical Quarterly, at 239, 240 (1913)

The Journal of the Washington State Constitutional Convention: 1889, at 501, n.20 (Beverly Paulik Rosenow ed., 1999)

Article I, Section 13: Habeas corpus.

The privilege of the writ of habeas corpus shall not be suspended, unless in case of rebellion or invasion the public safety requires it.

✢ ✢ ✢

> Next to personal security, the law of England regards, asserts, and preserves the personal liberty of individuals. This personal liberty consists in the power of locomotion, of changing situation, or moving one's person to whatsoever place one's own inclination may direct, without imprisonment or restraint, unless by due course of law. . . .

Thus did Sir William Blackstone, the great English legal scholar, describe the right against unlawful imprisonment protected by the writ of *habeas corpus*, or as it's often termed, the Great Writ. Literally meaning "you have the body," a writ of *habeas corpus* directs authorities holding a particular prisoner to present the court with evidence proving the imprisonment is lawful. It prevents the punishment of citizens who have not been found guilty of breaking the law, an injustice Alexander Hamilton called "the favorite and most formidable instruments of tyranny" in *Federalist* No. 84.

The language of Section 13 is nearly identical to the *habeas corpus* provision in the Oregon Constitution, reflects the language in Article I, Section 9 of the U.S. Constitution, and was adopted with little debate by the writers of Washington's constitution. Most of the convention attendees probably remembered the suspension of the writ of *habeas corpus* in 1886, triggered by riots of Seattle dockworkers who were upset over an influx of Chinese laborers. Matters came to a head when four dockworkers in a mob were shot by several guards escorting a large group of Chinese. Territorial Governor Squire declared martial law on the public grounds of combating the riots, but it appears the real reason was to prevent the arrest of the guards who had fired on the mob. Chief Justice Roger Greene (of the Territorial Supreme Court) asked the constable who was to arrest the men to wait for thirty minutes, during which time the justice petitioned the governor to declare martial law. He agreed, and by doing so suspended all civil actions, including arrest and search warrants.

The courts have been nearly unanimous in their handling of Section 13, applying the same rationale used in a state Supreme Court case decided just two years after the adoption of the constitution. Written by Chief Justice Hoyt (also president of the constitutional convention), the decision defined the protections of Section 13 very narrowly: a court presented with a writ of *habeas corpus* could review only the plain language of the judgment documents (*In re Lybarger*). If a prisoner were incarcerated under a judgment rendered by a court with jurisdiction over him and his type of offense, the writ had to be denied. The court couldn't inquire into the facts of the case or whether there were any error in how the court arrived at the judgment. So while a writ has been granted for improperly denying bail and for a judgment rendered without a jury (where that fact was noted on the sentencing documents), it was not granted for claims of trial errors not obvious from the actual judgment documents.

Later cases upheld the narrow scope of the *Lybarger* decision. In 1909, the state Supreme Court declared that the writ of *habeas corpus* "is not a writ of error. . . . We can only look at the record to see whether a judgment exists, and have no power to say whether it is right or wrong" (*Ex parte Newcomb*).

Section 13, however, doesn't prevent the legislature from expanding this narrow scope, which Washington legislators did in 1947 with a law allowing courts to review the facts behind a judgment for constitutional violations. But the legislature cannot weaken Section 13's protections. In 1993, several prisoners challenged as unconstitutional a law that set a one-year time limit on post-conviction appeals, which includes writs, arguing that Section 13 allowed for no time limit on the *habeas corpus* writ. The court agreed with that argument, but upheld the statute, because it included several broad exemptions allowing a writ of *habeas corpus* to be filed even after the one-year period.

Cases

In re Lybarger, 2 Wash. 131 (1891)
Ex parte Newcomb, 56 Wash. 395 (1909)
State v. Foster, 84 Wash. 58 (1915)
Grieve v. Webb, 22 Wash.2d 902, (1945)
Petition of Runyan, 121 Wash.2d 432 (1993)

Other Sources

Federalist Papers, No. 84 (Alexander Hamilton)
Wilfred J. Airey, *A History of the Constitution and Government of the Washington Territory* at 372–73 (unpublished Ph.D. dissertation, Volume II, 1945)

Article I, Section 14:
Excessive bail, fines and punishments.

Excessive bail shall not be required, excessive fines imposed, nor cruel punishment inflicted.

The Washington state prohibition on cruel punishments is nearly identical to the Eighth Amendment of the U.S. Constitution. There was some debate at the state constitutional convention whether to use the traditional phrase "cruel and unusual punishment" in keeping with the federal provision. One delegate in particular felt "unusual" should be inserted, noting his opposition to execution by electricity, but the convention determined that "cruel" was sufficient. Numerous other state constitutions (including three of the original thirteen colonies) omit "unusual."

The Washington Supreme Court has ruled that Section 14 affords greater protection for individuals than its federal counterpart. An independent analysis of both clauses is appropriate in claims of cruel punishment, but if the state provision is not violated, courts generally find no violation of the federal provision.

W. S. Gilbert wrote, "Let the punishment fit the crime," a credo Washington courts follow even today. Courts will find a violation of the prohibition on cruel punishment when the punishment is grossly disproportionate to the crime. If, in view of contemporary standards, the punishment would "shock the general conscience" and "violate principles of fundamental fairness," it is considered grossly disproportionate (*State v. Gibson*). A *harsh* punishment, "in the sense that it is strongly unpleasant to the person upon whom it is inflicted," does not rise to the level of cruel (*State v. Rose*).

Courts evaluate four factors when addressing claims of cruel punishment: the nature of the offense, the legislative purpose behind statute, the punishment the defendant would have received in other jurisdictions for the same offense, and punishment meted out for other offenses in the same jurisdiction.

Numerous court decisions have held that capital punishment does not constitute cruel punishment, and execution by hanging is not unconstitutional. In 1996, the Washington Supreme Court ruled in three companion cases that a life sentence without possibility of parole, mandated by the state's "three-strikes" law, was not an unconstitutionally cruel punishment. Additionally, a vasectomy operation performed on a perpetrator of child rape did not constitute cruel punishment prohibited by this provision.

A life sentence, however, imposed on a defendant whose "habitual offender" status was based on convictions for fraud totaling less than $470 was deemed cruel. Jail conditions may constitute cruel punishment where conditions are so base, inhumane, or barbaric as to offend the dignity of any human being.

Cases

State v. Feilen, 70 Wash. 65 (1912)
State v. Rose, 7 Wash.App. 176 (1972)
Woods v. Burton, 8 Wash.App. 13 (1972)
State v. Gibson, 16 Wash.App. 119 (1976)
State v. Fain, 94 Wash.2d 387 (1980)
Matter of Personal Restraint of Lord, 123 Wash.2d 296 (1994)

State v. Manussier, 129 Wash.2d 652 (1996)
State v. Rivers, 129 Wash.2d 736 (1996)
State v. Thorne, 129 Wash.2d 736 (1996)
State v. Morin, 100 Wash.App. 25 (2000)
State v. Yates, 161 Wash.2d 714 (2007)

Other Sources

The Journal of the Washington State Constitutional Convention: 1889, at 502 (Beverly Paulik Rosenow ed., 1999)

Article I, Section 15: Convictions, effect of.

No conviction shall work corruption of blood, nor forfeiture of estate.

✧ ✧ ✧

The odd wording of Section 15 makes it appear complicated at first glance, but in reality it protects a very simple individual right. Similar provisions appear in the federal and many state constitutions, written in reaction to the English practice of requiring convicted felons to forfeit their property to the English king. This practice was based on the idea that a criminal act was a breach of the public peace and justified taking away a person's right to own property. Not only did this rule punish the criminal, however, but it also prevented the criminal's heirs from ever inheriting their ancestor's property. When our founding fathers wrote the U.S. Constitution, they abhorred the thought of forcing innocent children to suffer for the sins of their forebearers, terming it "a great hardship" and even "rank injustice" (*State v. Young*).

Section 15 protects Washington citizens against this type of injustice, ensuring that conviction of a felony cannot result in "forfeiture" of the criminal's property or "corruption of blood," that is, the disinheritance of the criminal's heirs. With no exceptions, Section 15 is even more protective than the federal Constitution, which allows forfeiture of property during a criminal's lifetime, just not after his death. A retired police officer's pension, for example, cannot be taken away due to commission of a felony.

But the state Supreme Court has made it clear that Section 15 only prevents the forfeiture of property where simple commission of a crime revokes a person's right to own property. The section doesn't prevent forfeiture for other "rational and legitimate purposes," such as restitution, rehabilitation, punishment for the crime, or denying the criminal from profiting from a bad act (*State v. Young*).

For example, a person who kills his wife in order to obtain her property can have his inheritance taken away. The court felt that to grant the murderer the fruits of his crime "is so utterly opposed to justice, good conscience, morals, and the maxims of the common law which are a part of the law of the land in force in this state that we are utterly unable to assent thereto" (*In re Tyler's Estate*).

Cases

In re Tyler's Estate, 140 Wash. 679 (1926)
Leonard v. City of Seattle, 81 Wash.2d 479 (1972)
State v. Young, 63 Wash.App. 324 (1991)
State v. Weins, 77 Wash.App. 651 (1995)
State v. Devin, 158 Wash.2d 157 (2006)

Article I, Section 16: Eminent domain.

Private property shall not be taken for private use, except for private ways of necessity, and for drains, flumes, or ditches on or across the lands of others for agricultural, domestic, or sanitary purposes. No private property shall be taken or damaged for public or private use without just compensation having been first made, or paid into court for the owner, and no right-of-way shall be appropriated to the use of any corporation other than municipal until full compensation therefor be first made in money, or ascertained and paid into court for the owner, irrespective of any benefit from any improvement proposed by such corporation, which compensation shall be ascertained by a jury, unless a jury be waived, as in other civil cases in courts of record, in the manner prescribed by law. Whenever an attempt is made to take private property for a use alleged to be public, the question whether the contemplated use be really public shall be a judicial question, and determined as such, without regard to any legislative assertion that the use is public: Provided, That the taking of private property by the state for land reclamation and settlement purposes is hereby declared to be for public use. [AMENDMENT 9, 1919 p 385 Section 1. Approved November, 1920.].

Eminent domain is the power of governmental entities to condemn private property and convert it for a necessary public use. Washington's eminent domain provision was modeled on the Alabama and California constitutions. Amendment 9 (1920) added the clause allowing the taking of private property for reclamation purposes.

Consistent with the constitutional charge to "protect and maintain individual rights" (Article I, Section 1), the text of Section 16 is more expansive in its protection of private property than the federal takings clause. The provision specifically prohibits the taking of private property for private use, relegates the question of whether the use is truly public to the courts, and states that property shall not be "damaged" without compensation to the owner. Because of these differences, the Washington Supreme Court has said Section 16, when compared to its federal counterpart, "in some ways provides greater protection" (*Eggleston v. Pierce County*).

Washington courts have developed a three-part test to evaluate the exercise of eminent domain. In order to justify a taking, the government body must prove: (1) the use is really public, (2) the public interest requires it, and (3) the property appropriated is necessary for that purpose. But despite the strong mandate for protection of private property rights, court decisions have drifted over the last fifty years, allowing an erosion of the constitutional protection.

The constitution explicitly prohibits the condemnation of private property for private use, but courts have adopted conflicting and "chaotic" rules on what qualifies as a public use, as one law review put it. Early cases indicated the condemned property must be used *by* the public, not merely for a use that might "indirectly promote the public interest or general prosperity" (*Healy Lumber Co. v. Morris*). Courts have recognized that private and public uses may sometimes be inextricably combined, and condemned property may also include some private use that is merely incidental to the public use (*Chandler v. City of Seattle; City of Tacoma v. Nisqually*).

In 1963, the watershed case of *Miller v. Tacoma* allowed government entities to condemn property for public *purposes* (distinguished from public *uses*) and turn the property over to another private entity. Under the Urban Renewal Act, cities were permitted to declare certain areas "blighted," acquire and improve those properties, and sell the property back to private entities, all for the public "purpose" of urban renewal. In this case, Victor Miller's property fell within the boundaries of the urban renewal project and was condemned, despite being in good condition and well maintained.

Relying on a number of cases from other states, the state Supreme Court ruled that the condemnation of Miller's property did not violate Section 16. "The intent of the act was to acquire and prevent recurrence of 'blighted areas.' Experience has shown and the facts of this case indicate that the area must be treated as a unit and that a particular building either within or near the blighted area may have to be included to accomplish the purposes of the act." Justice Hugh Rosellini wrote a strong dissent in *Miller*, where he said: "One man's land should not be seized by the government and sold to another man so that the purchaser may build a better house, or enhance the beauty or aesthetic value according to the ideas of an artist or planner whose tastes have the sanction of the government. . . . Under our constitution, the government does not have this power."

In 1995, the Washington State Convention and Trade Center undertook an expansion project. The legislature approved funding, contingent on the Trade Center's securing $15 million from some other source. The Trade Center identified an expansion plan that extended an exhibit space that sat four stories above ground. The expansion would also sit four stories high, thereby necessitating condemnation of the surplus space below, which could be sold or leased in order to raise the necessary project funds. Several property owners on this tract of land challenged the proposal, arguing it was an impermissible condemnation for private use. The owners also argued that condemnation was not necessary, given the availability of other property. The Supreme

Court upheld the condemnation, noting the private use was incidental and not the "primary purpose" of the development.

Section 16 provides a check on the state's power of eminent domain by placing the question of what is a public use in the hands of the judiciary "without regard to any legislative assertion that the use is public." (This clause appeared in only two other state constitutions in 1889, Missouri and Colorado, and a motion to strike the reference to the legislature failed during the constitutional convention.)

Early decisions reflect the courts' disregard for legislative declarations: "under the provision of our Constitution, the court is untrammeled by any consideration due to Legislative assertion or enactment" (*Healy Lumber Co. v. Morris*); "it remains the duty of the court to disregard [a legislative] assertion if the court finds it to be unfounded" (*State ex rel. Andersen v. Superior Court*); "whether the use be 'really public' is for the courts to determine" (*Decker v. State*).

Over time, courts have developed a more deferential view of legislative findings. While the question of public use is ultimately a judicial determination, legislative declarations are now "entitled to great weight" (*Hogue v. Port of Seattle; HTK Management v. Seattle Popular Monorail Authority*).

Not only must the court determine whether the contemplated use is public, but there must also be a showing that the condemnation is necessary to accomplish the public use. Early cases cited a "universal rule" that governments should condemn no more property than the public use requires, and excess property is an unlawful condemnation (*City of Tacoma v. Humble Oil*). This protection is intended to prevent city authorities from engaging in profitable land speculation by condemning excess property for eventual resale.

Even this protection has been eroded by judicial bifurcation of legislative findings of "public use" and "necessity." In *HTK Management v. Seattle Popular Monorail Authority*, a Seattle transportation authority condemned a parcel of private property to be used as the site of a monorail station. While the station footprint would occupy only one-third of the parcel at most, the Monorail Authority argued the remaining portion was needed for a construction staging area. They adopted an internal plan to sell the remaining portion of the property to private developers after its use as a staging area was complete.

The Supreme Court upheld the condemnation as lawful. Despite the language in Section 16 limiting findings of public use to the judiciary, the court ruled that legislative determinations of necessity are "conclusive" absent some proof of fraud. Another ruling expanded this rule: "Even if the decision was partially motivated by improper considerations, it will not be vacated so long as 'the proposed condemnation demonstrates a genuine need'" (*Sound Transit v. Miller*).

This fraud standard is nearly impossible to prove, as discovered by the Strobel sisters in Burien. The City of Burien undertook an upscale development around property owned by the Strobel family, where the family operated a popular diner-style restaurant. The city launched condemnation proceedings, and the city manager told his staff to "make damn sure" a road went through the Strobel restaurant in order to justify the taking. The trial court judge acknowledged that the road could have been accomplished without affecting the restaurant, but reluctantly ruled in favor of the city, given the deferential standard mandated by previous court rulings.

In *Sound Transit v. Miller*, the Supreme Court ruled that municipal determinations of necessity could be made in near-secret conditions, where the only public hearing notice given to the property owner was on an obscure government website.

An unconstitutional taking can also occur when some regulation encumbers a private landowner's use of their property. Challenges to these regulatory takings review whether: (1) a regulation affects a total taking of all economically viable use of one's property, (2) the regulation has resulted in an actual physical invasion upon one's property, or (3) a regulation destroys one or more of the fundamental attributes of ownership (such as the right to possess, exclude others from trespassing, and to dispose of property); or (4) the regulations were employed to enhance the value of publicly held property (*Manufactured Housing Communities of Washington v. State*).

Cases

Healy Lumber Co. v. Morris, 33 Wash. 490 (1903)

City of Tacoma v. Nisqually Power Co., 57 Wash. 420 (1910)

Neitzel v. Spokane International Ry. Co., 65 Wash. 100 (1911)

Chandler v. City of Seattle, 80 Wash. 154 (1914)

Langdon v. City of Walla Walla, 112 Wash. 446 (1920)

State ex rel. Andersen v. Superior Court, 119 Wash. 406 (1922)

City of Seattle v. Faussett, 123 Wash. 613 (1923)

Decker v. State, 188 Wash. 222 (1936)

Hogue v. Port of Seattle, 54 Wash.2d 799 (1959)

City of Tacoma v. Humble Oil & Refining Co., 57 Wash.2d 257 (1960)

King County v. Theilman, 59 Wash.2d 586 (1962)

Miller v. City of Tacoma, 61 Wash.2d 374 (1963)

Petition of City of Seattle, 96 Wash.2d 616 (1981)

Orion Corp. v. State, 109 Wash.2d 621 (1987)

Presbytery of Seattle v. King County, 114 Wash.2d 320 (1990)

State ex rel. Washington State Convention and Trade Center v. Evans,
136 Wash.2d 811 (1998)
Manufactured Housing Communities of Washington v. State, 142
Wash.2d 347 (2000)
Eggleston v. Pierce County, 148 Wash.2d 760 (2003)
HTK Management L.L.C. v. Seattle Popular Monorail Authority, 155
Wash.2d 612 (2005)
Central Puget Sound Regional Transit Authority v. Miller, 156
Wash.2d 403 (2006)
City of Burien v. Strobel Family Investments, 133 Wash.App. 1018
(2006)

Other Sources

Richard L. Settle, *Regulatory Taking Doctrine in Washington:
Now You See It, Now You Don't,* 12 U.Puget Sound L.Rev.
339 (1989)
The Journal of the Washington State Constitutional Convention: 1889,
at 206, 505 (Beverly Paulik Rosenow ed., 1999)
Timothy D. Benedict, *Public-use requirement in Washington,* 75
Wash.L.Rev. 225 (2000)
Robert F. Utter & Hugh D. Spitzer, *The Washington State
Constitution: A Reference Guide,* at 31 (2002)
William R. Maurer, *A False Sense of Security: The Potential for
Eminent Domain Abuse in Washington,* Washington Policy
Center (2006)

Article I, Section 17: Imprisonment for debt.

There shall be no imprisonment for debt, except in cases of absconding debtors.

✜ ✜ ✜

Washington state's founding fathers could easily have been exposed to the practice of imprisoning debtors, especially the eleven delegates born in Europe where such actions were a longstanding tradition. But even the American-born delegates could have personally seen the ill effects of debtor prisons, as an 1831 newspaper investigation found at least 50,000 debtors imprisoned in the northern and mid-Atlantic states. So it was with firsthand knowledge that the delegates included Section 17 to clearly prohibit imprisonment for nonpayment of debts. History records only one objection to the section, from Delegate Trusten Dyer of Seattle (R), who was concerned that this Section "would allow men to escape imprisonment for unpaid [criminal] fines." But Delegate C. Warner, a resident of Colfax, assured him it would apply only to civil cases.

Section 17 has often been at issue in taxing disputes and in collections for personal injury cases. It was used to invalidate a jail sentence against a man who retrieved his car from a mechanic without paying for the repairs, but it didn't prevent a court from imprisoning a person who failed to provide detailed accounting documents on a real estate transaction.

Child and spousal support or alimony payments have also been a major source of Section 17 cases, usually involving jail sentences against a spouse not in compliance with a divorce order. One related question was quickly settled. In 1901, the Supreme Court unequivocally stated that "it is the well-settled law of this country that a[n] . . . order for alimony in a divorce proceeding is not a debt," and therefore Section 17 does not apply (*In re Cave*).

More difficult was the question of how to apply Section 17 to other parts of divorce orders, especially property settlements. For the first sixty years, Washington courts drew a bright line between property settlements and alimony orders, allowing imprisonment only for failure to pay alimony. But in a 6–3 decision in 1963, the Supreme Court blurred the line, decided that imprisonment was a proper remedy if there were a reasonable relationship between the property settlement and the duty to support the spouse and children. Subsequent cases have followed suit, reasoning that Section 17 "simply was not designed to thwart . . . the equity power and discretion of our divorce courts" (*Brantley v. Brantley*).

As in the alimony issue, most Section 17 cases have hinged on the definition of "debt." Does it merely refer to contractual obligations, such as a car loan, or does it also refer to court fines for personal injury disputes (torts), tax payments, license fees, and similar monetary obligations? In 1909, the court determined that "debt" referred only to contractual obligations and could never be applied to a court fine for fraud or the like. Six years later, the Supreme Court broadened Section 17 protections to cover personal injury cases, saying, "[T]he people in adopting the Constitution meant to prohibit imprisonment on judgments founded in tort" (*Bronson v. Syverson*). Imprisonment is also allowed for debts incurred by fraud, since the punishment is for the crime of fraud, not for being in debt.

The "absconding debtors" provision in Section 17 is meant to prevent people from fleeing the state to avoid court proceedings related to debts, but it only operates if the legislature enacts a law on the issue.

While the protections of Section 17 have been narrowed slightly by the courts in the area of divorce orders, overall the section continues to protect citizens against unlawful imprisonment for unpaid debts.

Cases

Burrichter v. Cline, 3 Wash. 135 (1891)

In re Cave, 26 Wash. 213 (1901)

Ex parte Milecke, 52 Wash. 312 (1909)

Hamilton v. Pacific Drug Co., 78 Wash. 689 (1914)

Bronson v. Syverson, 88 Wash. 264 (1915)

State v. Williams, 133 Wash. 121 (1925)

Austin v. City of Seattle, 176 Wash. 654 (1934)

Brantley v. Brantley, 54 Wash.2d 717 (1959)

Decker v. Decker, 52 Wash.2d 456 (1960)

Matter of Marriage of Young, 26 Wash.App. 843 (1980)

Rainier Nat. Bank v. McCracken, 26 Wash.App. 498 (1980)

State v. Enloe, 47 Wash.App. 165 (1987)

State v. Pike, 118 Wash.2d 585 (1992)

State v. Reid, 74 Wash.App. 281 (1994)

State ex rel. Daly v. Snyder, 117 Wash.App. 602 (2003)

Other Sources

The Journal of the Washington State Constitutional Convention: 1889, at 507 (Beverly Paulik Rosenow ed., 1999)

Article I, Section 18:
Military power, limitation of.

The military shall be in strict subordination to the civil power.

Among the grievances listed against King George III in the Declaration of Independence was the complaint of an independent military: "He has affected to render the Military independent of and superior to the Civil Power" (Utter). In response to the British practice of quartering soldiers without legislative authority, the Third Amendment to the U.S. Constitution prohibits the quartering of troops in private homes without consent of the owner, "but in a manner prescribed by law."

Washington's Article I, Section 18 uses language that is nearly identical to the constitutions of forty-eight other states subordinating the military to the civil power. Many constitutions link the state's military clause with the right to bear arms, including Pennsylvania (1776 version), Indiana (1816 version), and Oregon (upon which Section 18 was modeled). The Washington Constitution, however, separates regulation of the military from the right to bear arms (see Section 24).

In the only case discussing this provision, the Washington Supreme Court ruled that the use of the National Guard for a criminal home search did not violate Section 18, as at all relevant times the guardsmen were supervised by local law enforcement authorities.

Cases

State v. Valdobinos, 122 Wash.2d 270 (1993)

Other Sources

The Journal of the Washington State Constitutional Convention: 1889,
at 502 (Beverly Paulik Rosenow ed., 1999)

Robert F. Utter & Hugh D. Spitzer, *The Washington State Constitution: A Reference Guide*, at 32 (2002)

Andrew P. Morriss, "Quartering of Troops," in *The Heritage Guide to the Constitution* at 323 (Edwin Meese III, et al. eds., 2005)

Article I, Section 19: Freedom of elections.

All Elections shall be free and equal, and no power, civil or military, shall at any time interfere to prevent the free exercise of the right of suffrage.

✢ ✢ ✢

Section 19 is one of the few pieces of the Bill of Rights to evoke any recorded debate among the constitutional convention delegates. As proposed, the section read only, "All Elections shall be free and equal." During floor debate, Delegate Cosgrove, a lawyer from Pomeroy, asked what "equal" meant. Thomas Reed, a Republican from Olympia, replied it meant the same as "free." Despite this apparent duplication, the convention rejected attempts to change the word "equal" to "open" or "impartial."

But the confusion didn't mask the delegates' desire to ensure that the right to election integrity be preserved. When one delegate made a motion to strike the whole section, the others voted it down. Possibly in response to this, one of the convention leaders, Republican Delegate Buchanan from Ritzville, stated, "Something of this kind should be in the constitution somewhere, so I shall preserve this here [in Article I] until I see it somewhere else." Finally, Thomas Minor, a Seattle doctor, moved to add the second section, "and no power" (*Spokane Falls Review*).

Section 19 has been used to invalidate some elections, but generally the Supreme Court has upheld government's authority to regulate elections reasonably.

For example, the court has refused to interpret this section as a universal right to let people hold elections in whatever time or manner they chose. In 1925, several individuals filed a recall petition that included libelous statements and used Section 19 in their defense against criminal defamation charges. The court explained that Section 19 could not "prevent the application of criminal laws," and more broadly, "does not mean that elections and voters may not be regulated and properly controlled" (*State v. Wilson*). In 1980, the court determined the section also did not prevent a county council from endorsing an anti-pornography ballot measure, because such an endorsement "did not interfere with the free election process" (*King County Council v. Public Disclosure Commission*).

Individuals have, however, successfully used Section 19 to invalidate local land-use related elections. The first major case involved an irrigation district that was taxing landowners without allowing them to vote in the district elections, effectively forcing taxation without representation. The court struck down this scheme, in part, as violating the landowner's rights to "equal" elections (*Malim v. Benthien*). This decision developed into a rule that Section 19 permits limited qualifications on voters in special utility districts (1) when the activities are primarily nongovernmental and (2) where the election issues greatly impact a specific class of people, such as landowners within that district. But in light of the federal and state fundamental right to free and equal elections, such voter limitations must be narrow and are subject to a high level of judicial scrutiny.

The federal Constitution doesn't have a parallel provision to Section 19, but the U.S. Supreme Court has found an equal protection right to vote by pulling from various constitutional sections. But Washington's courts have consistently found that Section 19 provides greater protection than the federal Constitution.

The limits of that protection were tested in court after several contentious Washington elections in the 1990s and the early 2000s. One case challenged the election of a county auditor, because the candidate was in charge of counting the ballots for her own election. The court upheld the election because the plaintiff didn't follow the procedures of the election contest statute, determining that Section 19 doesn't allow voters to flaunt the statutory procedure. A second case concerned the contentious 2004 governor's race, which ended after two recounts with a 133-vote win for the Democratic candidate. A voter claimed that the practice of election officials marking, or "enhancing," ballots to make them machine-readable violated Section 19, but the court disagreed, holding that the practice didn't actually change votes.

The court also hasn't allowed Section 19 to be used to put candidates on a "perfectly similar footing" with each other, recognizing that election rules may advantage one candidate without actually depriving voters of any election rights. For example, rules that allow a candidate who garners the majority of the vote in a primary to appear unopposed on the general ballot aren't unconstitutional.

Cases

Malim v. Benthien, 114 Wash. 533 (1921)
State v. Bartlett, 131 Wash. 546 (1924)
State v. Wilson, 137 Wash. 125 (1925)
Reynolds v. Sims, 377 U.S. 533 (1964)
King County Council v. Public Disclosure Commission, 93 Wash.2d 559 (1980)
Foster v. Sunnyside Valley Irr. District, 102 Wash.2d 395 (1984)
Becker v. County of Pierce, 126 Wash.2d 11 (1995)
In re Coday, 156 Wash.2d 485 (2006)

Other Sources

"They All Talk," *Spokane Falls Review,* July 30, 1889
The Journal of the Washington State Constitutional Convention: 1889,
    at 508–9 (Beverly Paulik Rosenow ed., 1999)

Article I, Section 20: Bail, when authorized.

All persons charged with crime shall be bailable by sufficient sureties, except for capital offenses when the proof is evident, or the presumption great.

✣ ✣ ✣

Section 20 is modeled on bail provisions from the Indiana and Oregon constitutions. An early draft of the provision provided bail for "all prisoners," but the clause was replaced with "all persons charged with crime."

An early Supreme Court decision recognized the right of bail as "fundamental" (*State v. Jackschitz*). Bail serves several purposes: it relieves the state of the expense of incarcerating all accused persons, frees defendants from imprisonment in recognition of the presumption of innocence, and secures the appearance of the accused before the court. It is not intended as a revenue mechanism or a punitive fine.

Use of the term "capital offenses" means an offense for which a sentence of death "*may be* imposed," but not offenses for which death *must* be imposed (*Ex parte Berry*).

The right to bail attaches at the first court appearance, not at the time of charging. Thus, a district court's general order that domestic violence offenders be held in custody pending their first appearance did not violate Section 20. The court reached this decision in part by observing the amendment of Section 20 during the constitutional convention from "all prisoners" to "all persons charged with crime" (*Westerman v. Cary*).

Bail is only available pretrial. In *State v. Smith*, the Supreme Court expressly rejected the argument that Section 20 allows the bail and release of criminal defendants after conviction or pending appeal. Additionally, unless a statute expressly provides otherwise, courts are without power to grant bail to a convict held in detention as a suspected parole violator.

Cases

State v. Johnson, 69 Wash. 612 (1912)

State v. Jackschitz, 76 Wash. 253 (1913)

Ex parte Berry, 198 Wash. 317 (1939)

State v. Heslin, 63 Wash.2d 957 (1964)

January v. Porter, 75 Wash.2d 768 (1969)

State ex rel. Wallen v. Judges Noe, Towne, Johnson, 78 Wash.2d 484 (1970)

State v. Smith, 84 Wash.2d 498 (1974)

Westerman v. Cary, 125 Wash.2d 277 (1994)

Article I, Section 21: Trial by jury.

The right of trial by jury shall remain inviolate, but the legislature may provide for a jury of any number less than twelve in courts not of record, and for a verdict by nine or more jurors in civil cases in any court of record, and for waiving of the jury in civil cases where the consent of the parties interested is given thereto.

Jury trials are not merely "procedural formalities," but "a fundamental reservation of power" to the people. As the people retain ultimate power over the executive and legislative branches through the ballot box, they retain control over the judiciary through the jury box (*State v. Kirkman*). Despite having no counterpart in the federal Constitution, Washington's framers knew the importance of including Section 21, pulling its language from the Oregon, California, and Nevada constitutions. There was lively debate on the wording, however, started by Delegate Griffitts of Spokane Falls, who tried to strike the last part after "record." Two Republican delegates successfully opposed this, saying the twelve-juror requirement would prevent the problem of hung juries caused by just one or two disagreeable jurists. Various other amendments were offered; none were approved (*Journal*).

The Washington Supreme Court has found Section 21 to provide stronger protections than the U.S. Constitution, although it is a minor issue, since the federal provision, the Seventh Amendment, does not apply to states. The biggest debates have been on the meaning and scope of "inviolate," both in criminal and civil cases, and as to what constitutes waiver of the right.

Courts have used sources such as *Webster's Dictionary* to define "inviolate" as "free from change, pure, intact," meaning Section 21 provides the right of a jury trial to anyone who would have had it in 1889, when the constitution was adopted. So there was no right to jury trial in a case involving a candidate's right to an elected office, as the pre-1889 common law would not have granted a jury trial for that issue. But at that time, there was a right to a jury trial in murder cases, so the legislature or courts cannot change that right. Section 21 renders it inviolate. Some have criticized this approach as too inflexible to keep up with the evolution of legal theories. One *Harvard Law Review* article has likened it to "asking how the War of the Roses would have turned out if both sides had airplanes." But nearly all states with similar provisions and the U.S. Supreme Court use the same test.

In 1983, a Washington court set up a very narrow approach to interpreting "inviolate," requiring there to be an "exact common law equivalent" to a present dispute to find a right of jury trial (*State v. State Credit Association*). But six years later, the state Supreme Court broadened this, allowing for a "more flexible historical approach" in order to avoid interpreting this "essential right so that it slowly withers away" (*Sofie v. Fibreboard Corp.*).

The scope of Article 21 in criminal cases is pretty clear: defendants have a right to a jury trial, even for mere misdemeanors. By implication, criminal trials must be decided by a unanimous twelve-person jury. But courts will still use the pre-1889 common law to define the scope, as in a 1945 criminal case where the court found no right to a jury, because there were no disagreements about facts for a jury to review. Article I, Section 22 expands on a defendant's rights in a criminal trial (*Brandon*).

But Article 21 also has a civil trial component, in which the scope is harder to define. At common law, jury trials were allowed where a party had legal claims, that is, they wanted money for damages and/or penalties. In contrast, only a judge would decide cases where a party had "equity" claims, meaning they wanted the court to order the other party to act or not act in some way (injunctions, restraining orders, etc.). Washington courts have used this tradition to interpret Article 21, finding that in civil cases there is a right to jury trial only for legal claims, unless the right has been specifically granted by statute. In cases with both legal and equity claims, courts have broad discretion to determine if a jury trial is appropriate. In *Sofie v. Fibreboard Corp*, the state Supreme Court struck down a tort reform law, because it automatically limited jury awards of noneconomic damages (a legal claim), in violation of Article 21.

In order to waive the right to a jury trial, a party must be informed of his Section 21 rights and given at least ten days to change his mind. Even after that period, if a party decides he really does want a jury trial, a court can grant his request. Criminal defendants don't need to request a jury trial, but civil litigants do, so their inaction can act as a waiver of the right.

Cases

State v. Doherty, 16 Wash. 382 (1897)
Brandon v. Webb, 23 Wash.2d 155 (1945)
Brown v. Safeway Stores, Inc., 94 Wash.2d 359 (1980)
City of Pasco v. Mace, 98 Wash.2d 87 (1982)
State v. State Credit Association, 33 Wash.App. 617 (1983)
City of Seattle v. Williams, 101 Wash.2d 445 (1984)
Sofie v. Fibreboard Corp., 112 Wash.2d 636 (1989)
State v. Ortega-Martinez, 124 Wash.2d 702 (1994)

Westberg v. All-Purpose Structures Inc., 86 Wash.App. 405 (1997)
Nielson By and Through Nielson v. Spanaway General Medical Clinic, Inc., 135 Wash.2d 255 (1998)
State v. Smith, 150 Wash.2d 135 (2003)
State v. Kirkman, 159 Wash.2d 918 (2007)

Other Sources

Developments in the Law—The Civil Jury, 110 Harv. L. Rev. 1408 (1997)
The Journal of the Washington State Constitutional Convention: 1889, at 510 (Beverly Paulik Rosenow ed., 1999)

Article I, Section 22: Rights of the accused.

In criminal prosecutions the accused shall have the right to appear and defend in person, or by counsel, to demand the nature and cause of the accusation against him, to have a copy thereof, to testify in his own behalf, to meet the witnesses against him face to face, to have compulsory process to compel the attendance of witnesses in his own behalf, to have a speedy public trial by an impartial jury of the county in which the offense is charged to have been committed and the right to appeal in all cases: Provided, The route traversed by any railway coach, train or public conveyance, and the water traversed by any boat shall be criminal districts; and the jurisdiction of all public offenses committed on any such railway car, coach, train, boat or other public conveyance, or at any station or depot upon such route, shall be in any county through which the said car, coach, train, boat or other public conveyance may pass during the trip or voyage, or in which the trip or voyage may begin or terminate. In no instance shall any accused person before final judgment be compelled to advance money or fees to secure the rights herein guaranteed. [AMENDMENT 10, 1921 p 79 Section 1. Approved November, 1922.]

Section 22 provides for the rights of those facing criminal prosecutions: specifically, the right to appear in court, the right to counsel, the right to know the accusations charged with, the right to testify, the right to compel the attendance of witnesses on one's behalf the right to confront witnesses, the right to a speedy trial and impartial jury, and the right to appeal.

The provision is modeled on constitutional provisions from Oregon and Indiana, as well as the Sixth Amendment of the U.S. Constitution. The only alteration made to the text during the constitutional convention was to insert "and by counsel" after "the right to appear and defend in person" (this was later changed to "or by counsel" by Amendment 10). In 1922, Amendment 10 added the clause regarding the jurisdiction for offenses committed while traveling.

Courts have wrestled with the question of whether Section 22 as a whole extends greater protection for the rights of citizens than the U.S. Constitution. In *State v. Hopper*, the Washington Supreme Court stated that Section 22 and the U.S. Constitution (specifically the Sixth Amendment) contain the "same protection" for criminal defendants, and the court suggested the state constitution may even be *less* protective of defendants' rights.

More recently, however, several courts of appeal and the Supreme Court have offered guidance on specific clauses within Section 22. In some instances, the rights identified enjoy greater protection under the Washington Constitution: the right to self-representation (*State v. Silva*); the right to self-representation on appeal (*State v. Rafay*); the defendant's explicit right to testify, compared to the "implicit" right in the federal Constitution (*State v. Robinson*); the right to a jury trial (*State v. Hobble*); and the right to appellate review "in all cases" (*State v. Schoel*).

In other instances, Washington courts see federal and state protections as similar or equivalent: the right to an impartial jury when evaluating individual jurors' views on the death penalty (*State v. Brown*); the right to counsel (*State v. Medlock*); witness confrontation clauses (*State v. Foster*); and the fair-trial clause (*State v. Bone-Club*).

Cases

State v. Schoel, 54 Wash.2d 388 (1959)
State v. Gunwall, 106 Wash.2d 54 (1986)
State v. Hopper, 118 Wash.2d 151 (1992)
State v. Hobble, 126 Wash.2d 283 (1995)
State v. Bone-Club, 128 Wash.2d 254 (1995)
State v. Brown, 132 Wash.2d 529 (1997)
State v. Medlock, 86 Wash.App. 89 (1997)
State v. Foster, 135 Wash.2d 441 (1998)
State v. Robinson, 138 Wash.2d 753 (1999)
State v. Bradford, 95 Wash.App. 935 (1999)
State v. Dhaliwal, 150 Wash.2d 559 (2003)
State v. Silva, 107 Wash.App. 605 (2001)
State v. Sandoval, 137 Wash.App. 532 (2007)
State v. Rafay, 167 Wash.2d 644 (2009)
State v. Pugh, 167 Wash.2d 825 (2009)

Other Sources

"They All Talk," *The Spokane Falls Review*, July 30, 1889
The Journal of the Washington State Constitutional Convention: 1889,
    at 156, 512 (Beverly Paulik Rosenow ed., 1999)

Article I, Section 23:
Bill of attainder, ex post facto law, etc.

No bill of attainder, ex post facto *law, or law impairing the obligations of contracts shall ever be passed.*

This three-part guarantee was passed by the constitutional convention with no recorded debate, and is very similar to sections in the California, Oregon, and Indiana constitutions, as well as Article I, Section 10 of the U.S. Constitution. While most of the federal Constitution was applicable only to the federal government, the founding fathers saw these three things as such threats to liberty that they applied Section 10 to states, practically ensuring its inclusion in state constitutions.

The prohibitions on bill of attainder and *ex post facto* laws help prevent criminal punishments from being administered in an arbitrary or retroactive manner. On the civil side, Section 23 promotes the stability of contracts by removing the fear that they may become void or unenforceable because of future legislative actions. Because Section 23's language is virtually identical to Article I, Section 10 of the federal Constitution, Washington courts have interpreted both the same and often relied on federal court decisions.

A bill of attainder is a legislative act (a bill or resolution) that punishes a specific person or group of people without giving them a trial. England's Parliament had a habit of using these bills to go after political threats, and the founding fathers wanted to prevent that practice from spreading to the new republic. While Washington courts have dealt often with allegations of bills of attainder, they have rarely agreed with them. In some instances, this was because the law in question dealt with civil regulations, not with criminal punishments. Other cases involved laws that placed a burden on a specific group of people, but did not actually punish them, as in a city ordinance regulating the location of adult video stores. One case determined that a "three-strikes" law, in which offenders who committed three serious felonies were given a harsh sentence, was not a bill of attainder, because it did not remove the protection of a judicial trial and didn't designate a specific group of persons.

An *ex post facto* law is one that retroactively punishes someone for an act that, at the time it was committed, was not a violation of law. The prohibition wasn't controversial for America's founding fathers, who felt it obvious that such retroactive laws were "contrary to the principle of legality itself." Not because criminals have a right to less punishment, but because they have a right to fair notice of punishment at the time they committed the crime (*Heritage Guide*). It's pretty clear they intended the provision to apply only to crimes, and Washington courts have adopted that view.

A myriad of criminal defendants have challenged Washington laws as *ex post facto*, so the Supreme Court has developed a test based on the federal *ex post facto* cases. First, a court will look to see if a law is merely procedural, or if it makes a substantive change; second, if it is retrospective; and third, if it disadvantages the defendant by altering the standards of his punishment. Based on this, the court did not find a violation of Section 23 for a law requiring the registration of sex offenders or a law changing the amount of time courts had to set restitution. But a law that changed the standards for what constitutes murder, thus allowing prosecutors to change a defendant's charge from assault to murder, was in violation of Section 23.

Section 23's prohibition on impairing contracts focuses on the civil side of legislation and was based on a provision in the Northwest Ordinance that established the Northwest Territory under the pre-Constitution U.S. Articles of Confederation. It was a statement of public policy to preserve private rights of property from government interference. Both nationally and in Washington state, this clause has fostered much litigation. In the state, this has developed on a dual track: interference with private contracts and interference with public (government) contracts. Overall, the right must be balanced with a state's public health and safety obligations, so some level of interference is constitutional. For example, in 1908 the Washington Supreme Court upheld a regulation prohibiting private porters and the like from operating in railway stations (thus impairing a contract between such a person and a railway company), stating that the ordinance "is reasonable, [and] is a valid exercise of police power" (*City of Seattle v. Hurst,* 1908).

For private contracts, Section 23 prohibits legislative action that substantially hinders performance of the contract, but the person concerned must have relied on the portion of the contract affected by the new law and relied on the law as it stood when the contract was signed. But even when all that is true, if the contract concerns an activity already regulated, then the person is deemed to have known further regulation was possible. For example, a law regulating the location of adult video stores was not an impairment to the lease for the store space, because the operation of such businesses was already regulated when the lease was signed. Similarly, the right of landlords to evict tenants is regulated, so the legislature can further limit the right to evict without impairing rental agreements.

When reviewing laws that affect public contracts, the Supreme Court looks to see if the law substantially hinders performance of a contract, and then must decide if the hindrance is reasonable and necessary for a legitimate public purpose. Courts must review this type of case more stringently than with private contracts, because a state is essentially impairing itself. Based on this, the court has struck down an initiative limiting the amount of motor-vehicle fees governments could charge, since that made it difficult for a government entity to comply with bondholder contracts. A dissenting justice noted that this issue could have been solved using other contractual remedies, such as compensating bondholders, rather than by striking down the entire initiative.

Cases

City of Seattle v. Hurst, 50 Wash. 424 (1908)

State ex. rel. Hagen v. Superior Court of Thurston County, 139 Wash. 454 (1926)

State ex rel. Carroll v. Simmons, 61 Wash.2d 146 (1962)

Wash. Federation of State Employees v. State, 101 Wash.2d 536 (1984)

State v. Edwards, 104 Wash.2d 63 (1985)

Birkenwald Distributing Co. v. Heublein, Inc., 55 Wash.App. 1 (1989)

Margola Associates v. City of Seattle, 121 Wash.2d 625 (1993)

State v. Ward, 123 Wash.2d 488 (1994)

Caritas Services, Inc. v. DSHS, 123 Wash.2d 391 (1994)

State v. Manussier, 129 Wash.2d 652 (1996)

State v. Hennings, 129 Wash.2d 512 (1996)

World Wide Video of Wash., Inc. v. City of Spokane, 125 Wash.App. 289 (2005)

Pierce County v. State, 159 Wash.2d 16 (2006)

Other Sources

The Journal of the Washington State Constitutional Convention: 1889,
at 512 (Beverly Paulik Rosenow ed., 1999)

David F. Forte, "State Bill of Attainder and State Ex Post Facto," in *The Heritage Guide to the Constitution*, at 170 (Edwin Meese III et. al. eds., 2005)

Article I, Section 24: Right to bear arms.

The right of the individual citizen to bear arms in defense of himself, or the state, shall not be impaired, but nothing in this section shall be construed as authorizing individuals or corporations to organize, maintain or employ an armed body of men.

✤ ✤ ✤

Borrowing from the example of other state constitutions, this provision explicitly protects the *individual* right to bear arms, thereby precluding the debate that has accompanied its federal counterpart: whether the Second Amendment right to bear arms is merely a collective right conditioned on militia service.

During Washington's constitutional convention, an early draft of Section 24 only guaranteed the right to bear arms. Concerned with corporate use of Pinkerton detectives to quell labor disputes, however, the Committee on Preamble and Declaration of Rights inserted the "armed body of men" clause. The delegates objected to private groups of men operating as bodies of troops with no publicly accountable head. Twenty-five years after ratification, one academic observed that "no original clause introduced for the constitution is of more importance and more in accord with strict democratic principles" (Knapp, 267).

In 1907, the Supreme Court upheld the conviction of a man charged with organizing and employing an armed body of men after he transported them to a schooner to intimidate the captain and remove members of the crew. While the defendant contended the judgment violated Section 24, the court observed that a constitutional guarantee of certain rights does not place these rights entirely beyond the state's police power. Furthermore, "Armed bodies of men are a menace to the public. Their mere presence is fraught with danger, and the state has wisely reserved to itself the right to organize, maintain, and employ them" (*State v. Gohl*).

While the right to bear arms is guaranteed, it is subject to "reasonable regulation," as the Supreme Court said in 1945. "Reasonableness" is determined by (1) whether "the regulation be reasonably necessary to protect the public safety, health, morals and general welfare" and (2) whether the regulation is "substantially related to the legitimate ends sought" (*Second Amendment Foundation v. City of Renton*). Blanket prohibitions, however, will not be upheld. For example, an Attorney General Opinion indicated that a county, city, or town may not enact a general prohibition against the sale or possession of handguns within the limits of its jurisdiction.

In *Second Amendment Foundation*, an ordinance prohibiting possession of firearms in places where alcoholic beverages were served was upheld as constitutional. The court ruled that the right to bear arms is only "minimally reduced" by prohibiting guns in bars, while the law advanced a significant public safety interest by reducing intoxicated, armed conflict.

State law also prohibits carrying a weapon in a fashion that would cause alarm. A King County man was convicted under this statute after he was seen walking his dog in a residential area while carrying a semi-automatic military rifle with ammunition clip attached. The defendant argued the law constituted an effective ban on carrying weapons as it is unclear which weapons might cause alarm. The court ruled that the statute was "narrowly drawn to promote a substantial public interest" (public safety and preventing alarm), while balancing the individual right to bear arms (*State v. Spencer*).

It is well established that prohibiting felons from possession firearms is a reasonable regulation and constitutes no violation of the right to bear arms. However, a statute criminalizing gun ownership while the accused is free on bond awaiting trial was declared unconstitutional.

An interesting quandary arises when a defendant commits a crime and happens to own or possess a gun. The constitutional right explicitly applies to defense of one's self and defense of the state, so use of a weapon for committing a crime is not constitutionally protected. The Supreme Court has ruled that the right to bear arms ceases when the purpose of bearing arms is to further the commission of a crime.

But other cases make clear that mere ownership of a gun cannot be criminalized. In *State v. Rupe*, the prosecutor introduced evidence of the defendant's gun collection, none of which was used in the commission of the crime, to establish the defendant's dangerous nature and to justify the death penalty. The prosecutor argued that the defendant's guns were only good for one thing, "killing others in combat." On appeal, the defendant argued the evidence of his gun collection was irrelevant and intended to prejudice the jury against him. The Supreme Court agreed that constitutionally protected behavior cannot be the basis of criminal punishment. "We see no relation between the fact that someone collects guns and the issue of whether they deserve the death sentence." The court reversed the death sentence and ordered a new sentencing phase.

State law allows sentence enhancements when a defendant is armed with a deadly weapon during commission of the crime, and these enhancements are not unconstitutional. The defendant is considered "armed" during commission of a crime if a weapon is "easily accessible and readily available for use" (*State v. Valdobinos*). The state must establish a nexus between the weapon, the defendant, and the crime. Mere possession of a weapon, however, is not sufficient for enhancing a sentence.

A person with a loaded gun under his car seat during a heroin delivery was considered "armed" for purposes of sentence enhancement. But discovery of an unloaded .22 rifle under a defendant's bed was not sufficient. Neither was mere presence of a weapon, when a defendant was led handcuffed into a room and seated five or six feet from a gun kept inside a coffee table. More recently, however, the Supreme Court has allowed a looser application of the nexus rule in *State v. Schelin*. In this case, a defendant convicted of growing marijuana was standing at the foot of the stairs to his basement as police executed a search warrant. After his arrest, police discovered a loaded weapon approximately six to ten feet from where he had first been seen. A divided Supreme Court ruled that close proximity to the weapon at the time of arrest justified an enhanced sentence.

A dissenting opinion in *State v. Schelin* suggested that subjecting the right to bear arms to reasonable regulation under the state's police power (starting with *State v. Krantz*) is inconsistent with the text of Section 24, in light of other constitutional provisions that explicitly allow for regulation. For example: Ill. Const. art. I, § 22 ("Subject only to the police power, the right of the individual citizen to keep and bear arms shall not be infringed"); Ga. Const. art. I, § 1, para. VIII ("The right of the people to keep and bear arms shall not be infringed, but the General Assembly shall have the power to prescribe the manner in which arms may be borne"); Tex. Const. art. I, § 23 ("Every citizen shall have the right to keep and bear arms in the lawful defense of himself or the State; but the Legislature shall have power, by law, to regulate the wearing of arms, with a view to prevent crime"); Utah Const. art. I, § 6 ("The individual right of the people to keep and bear arms for security and defense of self, family, others, property, or the state, as well as for other lawful purposes shall not be infringed; but nothing herein shall prevent the legislature from defining the lawful use of arms").

The Supreme Court refined its analysis of gun regulations in *State v. Sieyes*. A seventeen-year-old, Christopher Sieyes, was convicted for unlawful possession of a handgun—state law generally prohibits minors from possessing firearms. The Washington Supreme Court held that the Second Amendment applies to the states (a holding later reached by the U.S. Supreme Court in a separate case) and also noted that the Washington Constitution explicitly guarantees the right to bear arms. The court declined to apply the traditional levels of scrutiny (strict, intermediate, or rational) to firearm regulation. Instead, the court said, it is appropriate to look to the constitution's original meaning, the traditional understanding of the right, and the burden imposed on an individual by the statute. Ultimately, the court held that Sieyes had failed to demonstrate that Washington's unlawful possession statute was an unconstitutional violation. The analytical shift articulated in *Sieyes* will likely affect future decisions about the right to bear arms.

Cases

State v. Gohl, 46 Wash. 408 (1907)

State v. Tully, 198 Wash. 605 (1939)

State v. Krantz, 24 Wash.2d 350 (1945)

Second Amendment Foundation v. City of Renton, 35 Wash.App. 583 (1983)

State v. Rupe, 101 Wash.2d 664 (1984)

State v. Sabala, 44 Wash.App. 444 (1986)

State v. Valdobinos, 122 Wash.2d 270 (1993)

State v. Spencer, 75 Wash.App. 118 (1994)

State v. Mills, 80 Wash.App. 231 (1995)

State v. Johnson, 94 Wash.App. 882 (1999)

State v. Krzeszowski, 106 Wash.App. 638 (2001)

State v. Schelin, 147 Wash.2d 562 (2002)

State v. Spiers, 119 Wash.App. 85 (2003)

State v. Sieyes, 168 Wash.2d 276 (2010)

Other Sources

Lebbeus J. Knapp, "Origin of the Constitution of the State of Washington," *Washington Historical Quarterly*, at 267 (1913)

Washington Attorney General Opinion, No. 14 (1982)

The Journal of the Washington State Constitutional Convention: 1889, at 153 (Beverly Paulik Rosenow ed., 1999)

Article I, Section 25: Prosecution by information.

Offenses heretofore required to be prosecuted by indictment may be prosecuted by information, or by indictment, as shall be prescribed by law.

Article I, Section 26: Grand jury.

No grand jury shall be drawn or summoned in any county, except the superior judge thereof shall so order.

✤ ✤ ✤

Criminal offenses may be prosecuted by the filing of an information or by grand jury indictment. Grand juries review evidence presented by a prosecutor to determine whether criminal charges are justified. During the constitutional convention, delegates rejected several proposals that would have specified the number of jurors and the periods of time for summoning jurors.

Washington courts do not recognize a superior method for initiating criminal action, and there is no state constitutional right to a grand jury indictment. In an 1891 case, a Thurston County prosecutor filed an information charging a man with the crime of seduction. Upon conviction, the defendant appealed, claiming the prosecution by information was an illegal procedure. Washington's territorial constitution of 1878 provided only for grand jury indictment, and the crime was committed prior to adoption of the 1889 constitution. The Supreme Court stated in *Lybarger v. State* that whether action is commenced by indictment or information, it is "simply a mode of procedure by which the defendant is brought formally before the trial court."

Numerous cases have since affirmed that either method for commencing prosecution is appropriate. The method used is entirely within the discretion of the prosecuting attorney, although the procedures for filing an information are to be determined by the legislature.

No violation of federal constitutional rights is committed when an information is substituted for a grand jury indictment. The requirement for "due process of law" as used in the Fifth Amendment of the U.S. Constitution was not meant to perpetuate the grand jury in all states.

Cases

In re Rafferty, 1 Wash. 382 (1890)
Lybarger v. State, 2 Wash. 552 (1891)
State v. McGilvery, 20 Wash. 240 (1898)
State v. Fisk, 151 Wash. 323 (1929)
Payne v. Smith, 30 Wash.2d 646 (1948)
State v. Beck, 56 Wash.2d 474 (1960)
State v. Westphal, 62 Wash.2d 301 (1963)
State v. Dunn, 70 Wash.2d 572 (1967)
State v. Platz, 33 Wash.App. 345 (1982)

Other Sources

The Journal of the Washington State Constitutional Convention: 1889, at 513–14 (Beverly Paulik Rosenow ed., 1999)

Article I, Section 27: Treason, defined, etc.

Treason against the state shall consist only in levying war against the state, or adhering to its enemies, or in giving them aid and comfort. No person shall be convicted of treason unless on the testimony of two witnesses in the same overt act, or confession in open court.

✤ ✤ ✤

Treason is a crime punishable by death, so defining the act is not something to approach lightly. While no debate was recorded between the Washington constitutional convention delegates over Section 27, they did use language carefully crafted by the American founding fathers to prevent any misuse of treason charges.

Section 27 was drawn from the nearly identical wording in the Oregon Constitution and Article III, Section 3 of the U.S. Constitution, among other sources. The language originated from a 1350 English law passed during the reign of Edward III, altered by American drafters to remove a provision allowing treason to be charged for "compassing or imagining the king's death," essentially allowing someone to be put to death for mere intentions. The founding fathers underscored their opposition to this by adding the requirement to prove an overt act of treason, language also included in Washington's constitution.

Federal courts have made treason hard to prove by interpreting the federal Constitution's treason clause very narrowly in such celebrated cases as that of Aaron Burr, who killed Alexander Hamilton in a duel. So in recent times, federal prosecutors have shied away from the difficult task of trying to prove treason, instead charging crimes such as espionage and terrorism even in cases when treason seemed obvious. For example, Ethel and Julius Rosenberg, an infamous couple convicted and executed for spying for the Soviets, were not convicted for treason, but for espionage.

The requirements for proving treason in Section 27 are an indication of how much the constitutional writers wanted to limit the use of treason charges. Washington courts have noted this difficulty, saying that the requirements for proving perjury "are the strictest known to the law, outside of treason charges" (*State v. Olson*).

While there are no actual treason cases in Washington, there have been in other states. Oregon had one case in 1922 involving the conviction of a member of a crime syndicate under a statute called the Syndicalism Act. The defendant argued the act was unconstitutional under the treason clause, because it allowed a finding of, in essence, industrial or economic treason without the constitutional protections of two witnesses or a confession. The Oregon Supreme Court rejected the claim, saying the treason clause does not prevent punishment of acts intended to subvert the government that have not actually ripened into full treason.

Cases

State v. Laundy, 103 Or. 443 (1922)
State v. Olson, 92 Wash.2d 134 (1979)

Other Sources

The Journal of the Washington State Constitutional Convention: 1889,
    at 514 (Beverly Paulik Rosenow ed., 1999)
Bradley C. S. Watson, "Treason," in *The Heritage Guide to the
    Constitution,* at 264–66 (Edwin Meese III et. al. eds., 2005)
Revised Code of Washington § 9.82.010

Article I, Section 28:
Hereditary privileges abolished.

No hereditary emoluments, privileges, or powers, shall be granted or conferred in this state.

✤ ✤ ✤

Reaffirming that all political power is inherent in the people, Section 28 expressly prohibits the granting of hereditary advantages or privileges. An emolument is defined as "Any advantage, profit, or gain received as a result of one's employment or one's holding of office." A privilege is "a special legal right, exemption, or immunity granted to a person or class of persons; an exception to a duty" (*Black's Law Dictionary*).

Section 28 is modeled on the constitutions of the United States (Art. I § 9: "No title of nobility shall be granted by the United States: and no person holding any office of profit or trust under them, shall, without the consent of the Congress, accept of any present, emolument, office, or title, of any kind whatever, from any king, prince, or foreign state"); Indiana (Art. I § 35. "The General Assembly shall not grant any title of nobility, nor confer hereditary distinctions"); and Oregon (Art. I § 29. "No law shall be passed granting any title of Nobility, or conferring hereditary distinctions").

This provision has generated almost no litigation. In the early 1980s, two individuals were denied crab-fishing licenses under a statute that restricted transfer of licenses endorsements to parent-child transfers or upon the death of the owner. The fishermen denied licenses argued the limitation on license transfers was a violation of Section 28. The court of appeals ruled that the statute was not an unconstitutional hereditary privilege, as the law did not require that licenses descend to the heirs of the original holder.

Cases

Weikal v. Washington Dept. of Fisheries, 37 Wash.App. 322 (1984)

Other Sources

Black's Law Dictionary (7th ed. 1999)

Article I, Section 29: Constitution mandatory.

The provisions of this constitution are mandatory, unless by express words they are declared to be otherwise.

✤ ✤ ✤

Section 29 demonstrates a concern on the part of Washington's constitutional writers that subsequent generations would misinterpret or abuse their work. Using what is known as a rule of construction, this section explicitly requires courts to interpret the constitution plainly, using the common and ordinary meaning of words as they were used in 1889 when the constitution was ratified.

While Section 29 has been quoted in dozens of cases, there are relatively few where it has been a central element of a case. The common theme in these cases is a government action that, while arguably good policy, violates the clear language of a constitutional provision. An early case involved a grant from Pierce County to a private county fair association, which the court found to violate two sections in Article VIII of the Washington Constitution that prohibit loans or grants to private parties. The county argued that the grant was for a *public purpose*, but the Supreme Court replied that "if the framers of the Constitution had intended only to prohibit counties from giving money . . . for other than . . . public purposes, they would doubtless have said so." Since they did not, Section 29 required the court to find the county's grant unconstitutional (*Johns v. Wadsworth*).

A 1954 case also invoked Section 29, this time to enforce obedience to Article III, Section 24, concerning the seat of government. The court used Section 24's plain language to require the governor and heads of state agencies to have offices in the state capital.

The mandate of Section 29 applies not only to the original language of the constitution, but also to its amendments. The Supreme Court made this clear when it used the plain language of the Sixty-Second Amendment (which prohibited governors from vetoing parts of bill sections) to invalidate Governor Booth Gardner's partial veto of a bill.

Section 29 also came up in a 1972 case about whether a city's depositing its funds in private bank accounts violates Article VIII, Section 7, which prohibits local governments from giving or loaning money to private companies. In a seeming departure from the *Wadsworth* decision, a majority of Supreme Court justices said no, but dissenting Justice Wright viewed Section 29 as requiring them to say yes. Taking the other justices to task, he said, "The majority takes much time discussing the safety of the investment. The wisdom of the provision was a decision for the framers of the constitution. We cannot substitute our judgment for theirs." Whether or not he was right about the outcome of that case, Justice Wright perfectly spelled out the intent behind Section 29 (*State ex rel. Graham v. City of Olympia*).

Joined with Section 1 (origin of political power), Section 30 (other rights reserved by the people), and Section 32 (fundamental principles), Section 29 helps maintain individual liberties as envisioned by the constitutional writers.

Cases

Johns v. Wadsworth, 80 Wash. 352 (1914)

State ex rel. Washington Nav. Co. v. Pierce County, 184 Wash. 414 (1935)

State ex rel. Lemon v. Langlie, 45 Wash.2d 82 (1954)

State ex rel. Graham v. City of Olympia, 80 Wash.2d 672 (1972)

Washington State Motorcycle Dealers Ass'n v. State, 111 Wash.2d 667 (1988)

Waremart, Inc. v. Progressive Campaigns, Inc, 139 Wash.2d 623 (1999) (R. Sanders, J., dissenting)

Article I, Section 30: Rights reserved.

The enumeration in this Constitution of certain rights shall not be construed to deny others retained by the people.

✠ ✠ ✠

A frequently recited principle is that our state constitution is a limitation upon, rather than a grant of, legislative power. But Section 30 states unequivocally that the individual rights enumerated in the Declaration of Rights are not exclusive. Other rights may be possessed and exercised by the people.

The Washington Supreme Court discussed this section in 1902, observing the universal recognition that "certain fundamental, inalienable rights under the laws of God and nature are immutable," and these rights cannot be violated by any legitimate authority (*State v. Clark*). The rights expressly declared in the constitution "were evidently such as the history and experience of our people had shown were most frequently invaded by arbitrary power, and they were defined and asserted affirmatively." The expression of these rights, however, does not preclude the existence of other fundamental rights. Hence the declaration in Section 30: "Apparently the expression that the declaration of certain fundamental rights belonging to all individuals and made in the bill of rights shall not be construed to mean the abandonment of others not expressed, which inherently exist in all civilized and free states."

Unenumerated liberties recognized under state and federal constitutions include "those privileges long recognized at common law as essential to the orderly pursuit of happiness by free men" (*Meyer v. Nebraska*). Those mentioned specifically in case law include the right to marry and to the care and custody of children, the right to travel, and the rights to teach, inquire, evaluate, and study.

The provision has its limits. A court declined in 1950 to rely on Section 30 to invalidate a contempt of court charge received by a defendant who refused to answer questions from a legislative committee about his involvement with the Communist Party. The parents of a defendant charged with first-degree murder refused to testify regarding conversations with their son about the charges and were cited for contempt. The court ruled that the right to privacy did not create a parent-child privilege under Section 30.

The Department of Corrections denied a journalist's request to videotape the execution of triple murderer Charles Campbell. The journalist filed an action with the Supreme Court, arguing that citizens have a constitutional right to attend executions, and journalists also have the right to videotape the proceeding, specifically citing Section 30 of the constitution. The court dryly disagreed that "attendance at an execution is the type of 'fundamental, inalienable [right] under the laws of God and Nature' which is protected. . . ." Absent this right, the journalist's claim that he had a constitutional right to videotape an execution was "unsupported" (*Halquist v. Department of Corrections*).

Cases

State v. Clark, 30 Wash. 439 (1902)

Meyer v. Nebraska, 262 U.S. 390 (1923)

State v. James, 36 Wash.2d 882 (1950)

State ex rel. O'Connell v. Meyers, 51 Wash.2d 454 (1957)

In re Luscier's Welfare, 84 Wash.2d 135 (1974)

Halsted v. Sallee, 31 Wash.App. 193 (1982)

Stastny v. Board of Trustees of Central Washington University, 32 Wash.App. 239 (1982)

State v. Maxon, 110 Wash.2d 564 (1988)

Halquist v. Department of Corrections, 113 Wash.2d 818 (1989)

Other Sources

Justice Robert F. Utter, *Independent Interpretation of the Washington Declaration of Rights*, 7 U. Puget Sound L. Rev. 491 (1984)

Louis Karl Bonham, *Unenumerated Rights Clauses in State Constitutions*, 63 Tex. L. Rev. 1321 (1985)

Article I, Section 31: Standing army.

No standing army shall be kept up by this state in time of peace, and no soldier shall in time of peace be quartered in any house without the consent of its owner, nor in time of war except in the manner prescribed by law.

✣ ✣ ✣

At the time of Washington's constitutional convention, it had been nearly a century since any American had been forced to quarter soldiers, yet the writers still included this subject in the constitution. It almost didn't make it in, as it wasn't in the text of Article I recommended by the Bill of Rights committee, but a Democratic lawyer from Dayton, M. Godman, successfully moved to add the section.

It is well that he did, for even though the idea of being forced to quarter soldiers is a strange one, it was a very real threat to the early American colonists. It would be a travesty if their struggle for liberty were forgotten through modern complacency.

Washington courts have not taken up Section 31, but two Oregon cases have cited that state's nearly identical provision. Both times it was as part of a discussion about individual gun rights (*see* Article I, Section 24), and both times the courts described the events that led to inclusion of the protection against standing armies. A catalyst was the reign of English king James II, which began in 1685. He created a standing army and required citizens to house the soldiers. After he was kicked out four years later, the throne of England was offered to William of Orange and his wife, Mary, on the condition that they sign a Declaration of Rights that included limits on standing armies.

During the years leading up to America's Revolutionary War, King George III required colonists to quarter British soldiers in their homes. Feeling common cause with the English citizens of 1689, America's founding fathers included prohibitions on standing armies in times of peace and on quartering soldiers in both the U.S. Constitution and many state constitutions.

Section 31 is a descendant of their actions, and while it has not been used yet, it provides a bulwark against the possibility of tyranny. As a constitutional scholar wrote shortly before Washington's 1889 convention, "It is difficult to imagine a more terrible engine of oppression than the power in the executive to fill the house of an obnoxious person with a company of soldiers, who are to be fed and warmed at his expense . . . and in whose presence . . . the civil restraints which protect person and property, must give way to unbridled will" (Cooley).

Cases

State v. Kessler, 289 Or. 359 (1980)
State v. Hirsch, 338 Or. 622 (2005)

Other Sources

Thomas M. Cooley, *Treatise on the Constitutional Limitations,* at
    375 (5th ed. 1883)
The Journal of the Washington State Constitutional Convention: 1889,
    at 516 (Beverly Paulik Rosenow ed., 1999)

Article I, Section 32: Fundamental principles.

A frequent recurrence to fundamental principles is essential to the security of individual right and the perpetuity of free government.

✤ ✤ ✤

This provision admonishes a frequent return to fundamental principles in order to preserve our system of free government and to secure individual rights. Only ten other states (including four of the original thirteen colonies) had used similar phrases in their constitutions by the time Washington attained statehood.

As noted by the Supreme Court in *Seeley v. State*, the wording of Section 32 was unique among state constitutions at the time of adoption. (Arizona and Utah subsequently adopted provisions modeled on Washington's Section 32.) Massachusetts and New Hampshire specified fundamental principles "of the constitution," while Washington added "the security of individual right" as the object of reviewing fundamental principles.

The first appearance of the "fundamental principles" phrase in American jurisprudence was the Virginia Declaration of Rights, written by George Mason in 1776, which stated, "That no free government, or the blessings of liberty, can be preserved to any people but by a firm adherence to justice, moderation, temperance, frugality, and virtue and by frequent recurrence to fundamental principles."

Section 32 is best understood when combined with the preamble ("We, the people of the State of Washington, grateful to the Supreme Ruler of the Universe for our liberties..."), Section 1 ("All political power is inherent in the people..."), and Section

30 ("The enumeration in this Constitution of certain rights shall not be construed to deny others retained by the people").

These provisions indicate that the constitutional delegates ascribed to the theory of natural (or fundamental) rights. (As noted by a 1992 law review, Section 32's sponsor, Delegate George Turner, subsequently offered statements as a U.S. senator that referenced his belief in natural law.)

Natural law is the theory that all men are granted inherent rights by the "Laws of Nature and of Nature's God." These rights are not conferred by other men or by a governmental system, and as a result cannot be taken away. As English philosopher John Locke wrote in his *Second Treatise of Government* (1689), all people are "equal and independent," and no one should "harm another in his life, health, liberty, or possessions."

America's founding fathers recognized natural law philosophy, as evidenced by the memorable phrase in the Declaration of Independence: "We hold these truths to be self-evident, that all men are created equal, that they are endowed by their Creator with certain unalienable Rights, that among these are Life, Liberty, and the pursuit of Happiness."

The influential legal scholar Thomas Cooley also cited natural rights when he wrote that a state's declaration of rights should include "[t]hose declaratory of the fundamental rights of the citizen: as that all men are by nature free and independent, and have certain inalienable rights, among which are those of enjoying and defending life and liberty" (Cooley, 45). Later, he observed that a constitution does not confer rights; it merely recognizes them. "In considering State constitutions we must not commit the mistake of supposing that, because individual rights are guarded and protected by them, they must also be considered as owing their origin to them. These instruments measure the power of the rulers, but they do not measure the rights of the governed" (*Id.*, 47).

The importance of Section 32 was noted by the Washington Supreme Court in 1994:

> It is often when government is most eagerly
> pursuing what it perceives to be the public inter-
> est that it is most likely to sidestep constitutional
> safeguards or to denigrate constitutional liberties.
> For precisely such reasons, our constitution wisely
> counsels us: A frequent recurrence to fundamen-
> tal principles is essential to the security of indi-
> vidual right and the perpetuity of free govern-
> ment.

The Supreme Court of Washington has cited the provision only thirty-nine times. Of these, only eighteen references are contained in the majority opinion. The remaining mentions are in dissenting and concurring opinions, which are not binding precedent, usually used as a prefatory reference for a histori- cal recounting of the issues at stake. For example, with a nod to Tennyson, Justice William J. Millard wrote in a 1943 dissent:

> The founding fathers were aware of the ills to
> which a republican form of government is pecu-
> liarly heir. They were mindful of the fact that a
> free people too soon forget the fathers' sacrifices
> which made the heritage of liberty possible, and
> that, through the years as they prosper, the people
> grow more indifferent to and heedless of, the
> fundamental principles of government and fall
> an easy prey to the slow and insidious encroach-
> ment from within upon natural and constitutional
> rights.

. . . the little rift within the lute
That bye and bye will make the music mute;
And, slowly widening,
'Ever silence all.'

The question, though, is how Section 32 applies in a practical sense. Is it merely a commentary on liberty, or is it a recognition of substantive rights not named in the constitution? As Justice Barbara Madsen observed in *Seeley v. State*, "Washington jurisprudence has yet to see a consistent approach to Article I, Section 32."

At a minimum, the Supreme Court has described the provision as an interpretive mechanism, where it is cited as a reason for analyzing principles supporting various rights. "Clearly, it is but an admonition not only to the legislature but also to the courts to constantly keep in mind the fundamentals of our republican form of government" (*Wheeler School Dist. v. Hawley*). In another case, the court declared it a "propitious time" to review fundamental principles, "considering the sweeping consequences" of a particular statute (*Dennis v. Moses*).

Washington courts have been reluctant to rely on Section 32 for substantive rights, but several justices and academics have argued persuasively that the provision is intended to expand and protect individual liberty. Justice Robert F. Utter wrote a concurring opinion in the *Southcenter* case, where he argued that the constitution is not the source of rights, but a recognition of them. "That the principles are not spelled out further indicates that the framers looked to other, nongovernmental sources for the origin of the rights listed in the constitution." If "rights inhere in the citizenry rather than emanate from the state," he wrote, the rights should be protected against infringements by other private parties and not just by the state.

In a frequently cited law review article, Brian Snure wrote

that Section 32 is more than an "abstract proposition," and the fundamental principles of liberty, democracy, natural law, and federalism should be used to expand the scope of individual rights protected by the constitution.

Cases

Dennis v. Moses, 52 P. 333 (1898)

Wheeler School Dist. No. 152 of Grant County v. Hawley, 18 Wash.2d 37 (1943)

State v. McCollum, 17 Wash.2d 85 (1943), reversed by *State v. Ringer*, 100 Wash.2d 686 (1983)

Southcenter Joint Venture v. National Democratic Policy Committee, 113 Wash.2d 413 (1989)

City of Seattle v. McCready, 123 Wash.2d 260 (1994)

State v. Rivers, 129 Wash.2d 697 (1996)

Seeley v. State, 132 Wash.2d 776 (1997)

Brower v. State, 137 Wash.2d 44 (1998)

King v. King, 162 Wash.2d 378 (2007)

Other Sources

Thomas M. Cooley, *Treatise on the Constitutional Limitations*, at 45, 47 (5th ed. 1883)

James W. Talbot, *Rethinking Civil Liberties Under The Washington State Constitution*, 66 Wash. L. Rev. 1099 (1991)

Brian Snure, *Frequent recurrence to fundamental principles: Individual rights, free government and Washington State Constitution*, 67 Wash.L.Rev. 669 (1992)

The Journal of the Washington State Constitutional Convention: 1889, at 517 (Beverly Paulik Rosenow ed., 1999)

Article I, Section 33: Recall of elective officers.

Every elective public officer of the state of Washington expect [except] judges of courts of record is subject to recall and discharge by the legal voters of the state, or of the political subdivision of the state, from which he was elected whenever a petition demanding his recall, reciting that such officer has committed some act or acts of malfeasance or misfeasance while in office, or who has violated his oath of office, stating the matters complained of, signed by the percentages of the qualified electors thereof, hereinafter provided, the percentage required to be computed from the total number of votes cast for all candidates for his said office to which he was elected at the preceding election, is filed with the officer with whom a petition for nomination, or certificate for nomination, to such office must be filed under the laws of this state, and the same officer shall call a special election as provided by the general election laws of this state, and the result determined as therein provided.

Article I, Section 34: Same.

The legislature shall pass the necessary laws to carry out the provisions of section thirty-three (33) of this article, and to facilitate its operation and effect without delay: Provided, That the authority hereby conferred upon the legislature shall not be construed to grant to the legislature any exclusive power of lawmaking nor in any way limit the initiative and referendum powers reserved by the people. The percentages required shall be, state officers, other than judges, senators and representatives, city officers of cities of the first class, school district boards in cities of the first class; county officers of counties of the first, second and third classes, twenty-five per cent. Officers of all other political subdivisions, cities, townships, precincts and school districts not herein mentioned, and state senators and representatives, thirty-five percent.

✤ ✤ ✤

Section 33 and its enacting provisions in Section 34 were passed in 1912 as part of the wave of populist and progressive sentiment that swept the nation around the turn of the century. This recall provision, coupled with initiative and referendum powers also passed that year (see Article II, Section 1), showed the people's distrust of government in general and the legislature in particular. While not part of the original constitution, this detailed grant of direct accountability to the people was in line with the many limitations the rest of the document places on the power of state government. For example, Article III dilutes the executive branch's power among eight elected officials.

At least three lawsuits were filed immediately to challenge the legality of Sections 33 and 34 over oddities in how the amendment was written and filed, but the Supreme Court held it was lawfully submitted and adopted by the people, becoming a binding part of the constitution. In one case, the court swept aside a claim of voter confusion by noting that the amendment and the subject of recall "was one of the public questions uppermost in the minds of our people . . . [for] a period of nearly two years" leading up to the election of 1912 (*Cudihee v. Phelps*).

In 1913, the state legislature enacted laws to govern recalls, as required by Section 34, but the laws were vague about what actions constituted good cause for a recall. Not surprisingly, this meant the courts fielded many Section 34 questions over the next sixty years, and some believed that recalls were being abused because the standards were so lax. In 1976 and again in 1984, the legislature tightened the laws to require more detail in the recall petition and a narrower definition of what constitutes malfeasance, misfeasance, or a violation of an oath of office.

While the statutory procedure for filing a recall petition is relatively straightforward, there has been some dispute as to the role of various parties in the process, usually because the elected official being recalled disputes the truth of the allegations and asks the county auditor or the courts to deny the petition. But the courts and the auditor are merely gatekeepers who ensure the sufficiency of the recall charges and the procedures followed, leaving it up to the tribunal of the people to decide the truth of the charges.

Unlike many of the eighteen states with statewide recall procedures, Washington allows recalls only if the petition includes charges of wrongdoing and those charges are determined by a court to be factually and legally sufficient.

Section 34 specifically requires charges of misfeasance, malfeasance, or a violation of an official's oath of office. Courts have interpreted "misfeasance" and "malfeasance" as "comprehensive terms" including "any wrongful conduct that affects, interrupts, or interferes with the performance of official duty" and violation of an oath as a failure to perform office duties "honestly, faithfully, and to the best of [one's] ability" (*Bocek v. Bayley*). These definitions were codified by the legislature in 1984 and must be interpreted in favor of the voter, not the official. Recall petitions should be based on facts, but the petitioner need not have firsthand knowledge of those facts, and a superior court can correct from supplemental sources the summary of the charges on the petition.

Part of the impetus behind the 1984 legislative change was to cut down on use of the recall process to harass government officials, so the legislature mandated that a superior court must always review the sufficiency of the allegations. The courts interpreted this to mean that allegations must be factually sufficient, containing enough facts that, if true, would indicate an unlawful act was committed, and legally sufficient, meaning the allegation couldn't be for a discretionary act. For example, in 2000, a recall petition was filed against the auditor of Pierce County, alleging she had lied under oath about her educational qualifications (malfeasance) and hadn't sent out postage-paid return ballot envelopes for a special election to approve funding for Qwest Field (violation of oath). The Supreme Court agreed there were sufficient facts to allege malfeasance for false swearing, but no misconduct for not sending postage-paid envelopes, as that decision was within the auditor's discretion.

In other words, if an official has legal justification for an action, they can't be recalled for that action. A drainage commissioner could not be recalled for seeking an anti-harassment order to exclude two neighbors from commission meetings, because he had a justifiable reason: fear of attack from his neighbors.

Sections 33 and 34 have been used often in their nearly hundred-year history and still remain a viable tool for citizens to hold government officials directly accountable. But the legislative changes in 1984 and the cases since then have increased the difficulty of filing successful recall petitions. A dissenting justice in a 2005 decision about the recall of a Spokane mayor cautioned that "constitutional rights do not submit to red tape," meaning the courts and legislature must be careful not to regulate the right of recall out of existence (*In re Recall of West*).

Cases

State ex rel. Lynch v. Fairley, 1913
Cudihee v. Phelps, 76 Wash. 314 (1913)
Tabor v. Walla Walla, 77 Wash. 579 (1914)
Chandler v. Otto, 103 Wash.2d 268 (1984)
Bocek v. Bayley, 81 Wash.2d 831 (1973)
In re Recall of Pearsall-Stipek, 141 Wash.2d 756 (2000)
In re Recall Charges Against Feetham, 149 Wash.2d 860 (2003)
In re Recall of West, 155 Wash.2d 659 (2005)
In re Recall of Carkeek, 156 Wash.2d 469 (2006)

Other Sources

Joshua Osborne-Klein, *Electoral recall in Washington state and California: California needs stricter standards to protect elected officials from harassment,* 28 Sea. L. Rev. 145 (2004)
Revised Code of Washington § 29.82

Article I, Section 35: Victims of crimes – rights.

Effective law enforcement depends on cooperation from victims of crime. To ensure victims a meaningful role in the criminal justice system and to accord them due dignity and respect, victims of crime are hereby granted the following basic and fundamental rights.

Upon notifying the prosecuting attorney, a victim of a crime charged as a felony shall have the right to be informed of and, subject to the discretion of the individual presiding over the trial or court proceedings, attend trial and all other court proceedings the defendant has the right to attend, and to make a statement at sentencing and at any proceeding where the defendant's release is considered, subject to the same rules of procedure which govern the defendant's rights, in the event the victim is deceased, incompetent, a minor or otherwise unavailable, the prosecuting attorney may identify a representative to appear to exercise the victim's rights. This provision shall not constitute a basis for error in favor of a defendant in a criminal proceeding nor a basis for providing a victim or the victim's representative with court appointed counsel.

Section 35 is a relative newcomer to the Bill of Rights, having been enacted via Amendment 84 in 1989. Proposed by Attorney General Ken Eikenberry and supported by victim's rights organizations and law enforcement officials, the amendment was passed unanimously by the legislature and approved by 78 percent of voters in the 1989 general election.

Backers of Amendment 84 intended to counter a perceived lack of public faith in the criminal justice system caused by the expansion of constitutional rights of criminals at the expense of their victims. Establishing constitutional rights for victims would restore a sense of equal justice. Some proponents also felt it would encourage victims of sexual assault crimes to report their attackers. The only criticism aired was that the amendment didn't go far enough to protect victims.

In essence, Section 35 allows victims to be involved in the trial process, and it's the scope of that role that has been at issue in two Supreme Court cases.

The first was decided in 1995 and involved a defendant who was charged with killing a twelve-year-old girl and sentenced to death. During trial, the court allowed the girl's father to make a statement about the impact of his daughter's death, which the defendant argued should have been excluded by constitutional due process protections for capital punishment cases.

But in 1991 the U.S. Supreme Court had decided that no federal constitutional provisions barred victim impact statements. Under that freedom, the Washington Supreme Court determined the state constitutional due process protections (Article 1, Sections 3 and 14) didn't prevent victim statements at trial. "Although defendants in capital cases have always had substantial due process rights," the court said, "the victim also now has constitutional rights."

While conceding that victim statements must be relevant, the justices strongly supported the relevancy of statements such as that made by the girl's father: "The loss to the family of the defendant if he is sentenced to death has been allowed to be considered. . . . [S]urely the loss to the innocent victim's family must be at least as relevant."

Six years later, the Supreme Court again took up a Section 35 question, this time in a case where a husband killed his wife and wanted the court to allow a statement from his father-in-law. The trial court said no, and the defendant claimed a violation of Section 35. The Supreme Court disagreed, explaining that the right to make a victim statement belongs to the victim, not the defendant. The lower court could have allowed the father-in-law to speak, but not doing so wasn't grounds to reverse the man's criminal sentence.

Two recent court of appeals cases have further defined the scope of Section 35. One clarified that a court can allow both the victim's family and the family's attorney to speak in court and can allow both oral and written victim impact statements. The other case determined that if a victim chooses not to speak and does not ask for help in making a statement, the prosecutor doesn't have a right to speak on the victim's behalf.

Cases

State v. Gentry, 125 Wash.2d 570 (1995)

State v. Stenson, 132 Wash.2d 668 (1997)

State v. Lindahl, 114 Wash.App. 1 (2002)

State v. Carreno-Maldonado, 135 Wash.App. 77 (2006)

Other Sources

Final Bill Report of the Senate Committee on Law & Justice and the House Committee on Judiciary for SJR 8200, 50th Sess. (Wa. 1989)

Bill Report of the House Committee on Judiciary for SJR 8200, 50th Sess. (Wa. 1989)

Bibliography

Airey, Wilfred J. *A History of the Constitution and Government of Washington Territory* (1945) (unpublished Ph.D. dissertation, University of Washington)

Beardsley, Arthur S. *Sources of the Washington State Constitution*, reprinted in 1987-88 Washington Legislative Manual (1987)

Benedict, Timothy D. *Public-use requirement in Washington*, 75 Wash. L. Rev. 225 (2000)

Bill Report of the House Committee on Judiciary for SJR 8200, 50th Sess. (Wa. 1989)

Black's Law Dictionary (7th ed. 1999)

Bonham, Louis Karl. *Unenumerated Rights Clauses in State Constitutions*, 63 Tex. L. Rev. 1321 (1985)

Coke, Sir Edward. *Institutes of the Laws of England* (6th ed. 1681)

Cooley, Thomas M. *Treatise on the Constitutional Limitations* (5th ed. 1883)

Developments in the Law—The Civil Jury, 110 Harv. L. Rev. 1408 (1997)

Final Bill Report of the Senate Committee on Law & Justice and the

House Committee on Judiciary for SJR 8200, 50th Sess. (Wa. 1989)

Fitts, James Leonard. *The Washington Constitutional Convention of 1889* (1951) (unpublished master's thesis, University of Washington)

Forte, David F. "State Bill of Attainder and State Ex Post Facto," in *The Heritage Guide to the Constitution,* at 170 (Edwin Meese III et. al. eds., 2005)

Hamilton, Alexander. *The Federalist Papers,* No. 84 (1788)

Hill, W. Lair. "A Constitution Adapted to the Coming State," *The Morning Oregonian,* July 4, 1889.

Hoffman, Jonathan M. *By the course of the law: Origins of the open courts clause of state constitutions.* 74 Or. L. Rev. 1279 (1995)

Hosford Katie. *The search for a distinct religious-liberty jurisprudence under the Washington state constitution,* 75 Wash. L. Rev. 643 (2000)

Index Digest of State Constitutions, Columbia University (2nd ed., Oceana Press Inc., 1959)

Madison, James. *The Federalist Papers,* No. 45 (1788)

Kinnear, John R. *Notes on the Constitutional Convention,* 4 Washington Historical Quarterly 276 (1913)

Knapp, Lebbeus J. *Origin of the Constitution of the State of Washington,* 4 Washington Historical Quarterly 227 (1913)

Maurer, William R. *A False Sense of Security: The Potential for Eminent Domain Abuse in Washington,* Washington Policy Center (2006)

Morriss, Andrew P. "Quartering of Troops," in *The Heritage Guide to the Constitution* at 323 (Edwin Meese III, et al. eds., 2005)

Osborne-Klein, Joshua. *Electoral recall in Washington state and California: California needs stricter standards to protect elected officials from harassment,* 28 Sea. L. Rev. 145 (2004)

Pitler, Sanford E. *The Origin and Development of Washington's Independent Exclusionary Rule: Constitutional Right and Constitutionally Compelled Remedy,* 61 Wash. L. Rev. 459 (1986)

"Red Hot Debates and Windy Oratory Prevails Throughout the Sessions," *Tacoma Morning Globe,* July 30, 1889

Rosenow, Beverly P., ed. *The Journal of the Washington State Constitutional Convention 1889,* with Analytical Index by Quentin Shipley Smith (Book Publishing Co., 1962)

Settle, Richard L. *Regulatory Taking Doctrine in Washington: Now You See It, Now You Don't,* 12 U. Puget Sound L. Rev. 339 (1989)

Sheldon, Charles H. *A century of judging: a political history of the Washington Supreme Court* (University of Washington Press, 1988)

Snure, Brian. *Frequent recurrence to fundamental principles: Individual rights, free government and Washington State Constitution,* 67 Wash. L. Rev. 669 (1992)

Stiles, Theodore L. *The Constitution of the State and Its Effects Upon Public Interests,* 4 Washington Historical Quarterly 281 (1913)

"Still Fooling Away Time Without a Pretense of Work," *Tacoma Morning Globe,* August 1, 1889

Talbot, James W. *Rethinking Civil Liberties Under The Washington State Constitution,* 66 Wash. L. Rev. 1099 (1991)

"They All Talk," *Spokane Falls Review,* July 30, 1889

Utter, Robert F. and Hugh D. Spitzer. *The Washington State Constitution: A Reference Guide* (Greenwood Press 2002)

Utter, Robert F. *Independent Interpretation of the Washington Declaration of Rights,* 7 U.Puget Sound L.Rev. 491 (1984)

Washington Attorney General Opinion, No. 14 (1982)

Watson, Bradley C. S. "Treason," in *The Heritage Guide to the Constitution,* at 264-266 (Edwin Meese III et. al. eds., 2005)

Afterword

While the seventy-five delegates who gathered in Olympia in 1889 did a masterful job of creating a government that would protect the rights of individuals, their work can easily be undone by a lack of knowledge and understanding.

When the Washington Constitution exhorts a "frequent recurrence to fundamental principles," we suspect the delegates intended not merely a review of the rights identified in the constitution, but an understanding of the nature and source of those liberties. Where do rights come from? What is government's role in creating or granting new rights?

The understanding of where rights originate has drifted over time—an example of which is found embedded in the Washington Constitution.

As discussed in this book, the delegates who penned the constitution's original text included several references to the theory of natural law. The preamble thanks the Supreme Ruler of the Universe for the liberties we enjoy, and the text later stresses that all power is inherent in the people, with government deriving its legitimate powers from the people's consent.

One hundred years after the ratification of the Washington Constitution, the state apparently veered away from this understanding. Amendment 84 was approved by the legislature, ratified by the people, and codified as Article I, Section 35. The amendment states the goal of meaningful participation in the criminal justice system by the victims of a crime. The section states: "Victims of crime are hereby granted the following basic and fundamental rights."

Amendment 84 was no doubt well-intentioned, but its language betrays a confusion about the nature of fundamental rights.

In 1913, Lebbeus J. Knapp wrote in his important thesis "Origins of the Constitution of the State of Washington" that fundamental rights are more than political favors or privileges granted by a legislature.

Writing of the Declaration of Rights, Knapp said:

> The declarations contained therein are brief, general, and comprehensive declarations of the rights of individuals which are deemed to be sacred. These rights are, by common understanding, considered to be inherent in the constitution of things, and are based on principles which no government can rightfully deny, and the assertion of them in constitutional provisions is not supposed to add materially to the tenure by which they are held.

In other words, while the legislature can grant or confer certain rights or privileges, *fundamental* rights are of a different character. Fundamental rights are not created by a governmental institution, but are recognized as inherent in each man and woman.

It is our hope that this book will point the readers toward a better understanding of the source of our liberties, and the state's role in protecting those liberties.